NUMINOUSNEOISM™ ART

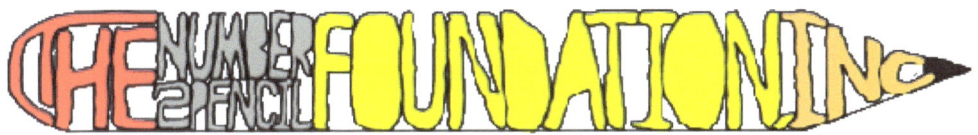

www.thenumber2pencil.com

A Real True-Story

THE BLACK-ARTIST TALE

Simple-Things Are The First-Part Of Great-Things

The Number 2 Pencil Foundation, Inc.
3550-#536 Grandview Parkway
Birmingham, AL 35243
www.thenumber2pencil.com

ISBN 978-0-615-83502-0

Cover Art and Design by Author: The Black-Artist John Solomon Sandridge (aka "Immortal-Black-Boy")

Printed: 2013 in the U.S.A.
The Number 2 Pencil Foundation, Inc. (501)(C)(3)

"Children and Teenagers 'Will Save
Their Own Future' if we S<u>HOW</u>
Them HOW to use their
IMAGINATIONS and
The REAL-MAGIC that's inside them."

-The Black-Artist John Solomon
Sandridge (aka "Immortal-Black-Boy")

Author and Illustrator

The Black-Artist John Solomon
Sandridge (aka "Immortal-Black-Boy")

PLEASE BE ADVISED: The following is a real true-story that contains NEW-WORDS. The words are made-up by The Black-Artist John Solomon Sandridge (aka " Immortal-Black-Boy"*). These words will cause your brain to work in genius-mode and your mind will think deep-thoughts. Your brain and mind will search for greater-meaning and super-understanding of Life. Each new-word has a * after it, and the meanings are at the end of the book.

My Wish Dream and Gratitude

I wish My-Smiles could "<u>Hug Every Child and Teenager</u>."

My dream is to S<u>HOW</u> Children and Teenagers HOW to DEVELOP their Greatest-God-Gift, which is an African inheritance called . . . *IMAGINATION.*

I'm grateful for my IMAGINATION. Since I was a Child and a Teenager I've used the NO. 2 Pencil and IMAGINATION and REAL-MAGIC to create and invent and discover magically-miraculous* ways to live an Artist-Life.

I wish and dream and am grateful that Children and Teenagers "Will Save Their Own Future" from *The Nasty-Stuff-Family**. This family was created by *Adult-Greed**. Its family members are Father-Pollution, Mother-Poverty, Sister-Sickness, and Brother-War.

If we accomplish what's possible it's done by us and for us. If we accomplish what is impossible it's done in us and through us by THE CREATOR OF LIFE, for all people.
  -The Black-Artist John Solomon Sandridge (aka
                              "Immortal-Black-Boy")

INTRODUCTION

I have A-QUESTION.

THE-QUESTION: is it true <u>*"All Things Are Possible"*</u>?
THE-ANSWER: ????
I'll share the answer with you soon, but how soon depends on how fast you read. Before you get The-Answer to The-Question, you need to know 2-things. 1) The Adult part of me is writing this book. 2) The Child and Teenager <u>parts</u> are telling my tale.
So . . . "I Know What I Know."

There's a Bible verse that says, "All Things Are Possible." Many Adults *believe* it's true, and it may be easy for them to *just* believe. As Children and Teenagers you need to believe it's true. But most of you have reasons *not* to believe it's true.

Like most Children and Teenagers you probably believe what you *see*, and that's what you <u>know</u>. Because most don't have healthy food and clean water and clean clothes and a safe home, what you see *shows* that *"Most Things Are Impossible."* And each *impossible* adds up to *Impossibles**.

As Children and Teenagers you can't *just* believe. You need magic to show that "All Things Are Possible" for you TO-BE* and TO-DO* and

TO-HAVE*.

Some Adults tell Children and Teenagers, "You should know magic isn't real." But there is a magic that is real. It's called *REAL-MAGIC*.*

REAL-MAGIC is in the minds and he<u>arts</u> and brains of all Children and Teenagers. It comes out of you as . . . *IMAGINATION*.

People who created and invented and discovered the computer and Internet and cars and houses and boats and planes and made Art used their REAL-MAGIC and IMAGINATION.

THE CREATOR OF LIFE (God) put REAL-MAGIC and IMAGINATION in the he<u>arts</u> and minds and brains of "The-First" people to live on earth. These people were The Original Black-Africans. Because IMAGINATION was put in them *first*, they passed it on to the Red-People and Yellow-People and White-People. So you, and all Children and Teenagers, have REAL-MAGIC and IMAGINATION.

But wait!

You can't *just* be told you have REAL-MAGIC and IMAGINATION. You must be *SH<u>OWN</u>* that you have both and be taught HOW to get it to come out. The fun way for you to let these gifts out is by using a power-filled* NO. 2 Pencil. When it's used to draw and write, *Impossibles* can be turned into . . . *I'm-Possible*.*

The I'm-Possible attitude is inside a blue-green gland at the very tip of your he<u>art</u>. Doctors and scientists and teachers and Adults don't know about this gland. The reason they don't know is because it's 1,000,000-billion times smaller than the point of a pin. Yet this teeny-tiny gland is the most power-full* gland in your body. It's so power-full it can *push* you to want TO-BE "The-First" person TO-DO new things that have *Never-Ever-Been-Done* before and *Never-Ever-Been-Heard* before and *Never-Ever-Been-Seen* before. And this means before never can become ever, which would be "The-First" time nothing becomes everything and all things before there ever was *The-Now*.*

I know this is true because I am "The-First" person to know about this bright blue-green gland. Since I'm "The First" to know about it, I named it the . . . *Connatural-Desire Gland*.*

The first time my Connatural-Desire Gland *pushed* me, I was an 8-year-old child who did something special. For "The-First" time ever, I used my I'm-Possible attitude. The way I did this was by using a power-filled NO. 2 Pencil and REAL-MAGIC and my IMAGINATION. And I was able TO-DO what no one in my family had Never-Ever-Done before.

This is why I say, "I KNOW WHAT I KNOW." I <u>know</u> I'm supposed to do really important things with Art. And I'm supposed to

S<u>HOW</u> Children and Teenagers HOW to use the NO. 2 Pencil and their REAL-MAGIC and IMAGINATION to create and invent and discover GOoD* ways to live so that "They Will Save Their Own Future."

THE-ANSWER to THE-QUESTION at the beginning of the introduction is . . . *Yes!*

"All Things Are Possible" for Children and Teenagers who want to BE-come* what they BE-lieve* (BE-live). All Children and Teenagers *should* have clean water and healthy food and clean clothes, and *they deserve TO-HAVE all of it . . . today!*

A VERY SPECIAL ORGANIZATION

My Friends and I have created a very special organization. The name of the organization is *The Number 2 Pencil Foundation, Inc.* (501) (C)(3). We will use it to S<u>HOW</u> Children and Teenagers HOW to use the *NO. 2 Pencil* and use REAL-MAGIC to develop *IMAGINATION.* They will create and invent and discover drawings and paintings and collages and sculptures and poems and stories and music and dances and songs and movies and technologies no one has Never-Ever-Seen and Never-Ever-Done and Never-Ever-Heard before, and "They Will Save Their Own Future."

When Children and Teenagers use a NO. 2 Pencil to draw and write, they use the front of their brain, and it has 3-p<u>arts</u>: the right and left and bottom.

The left front-side of the brain is the p<u>art</u> that says, "*I will.*" When you use it you have positive-feelings and <u>learn</u> TO-BE creative and invent and discover new things.

The right front-side of the brain is the p<u>art</u> that says, "*I won't.*" When you use it you have clear thinking and good judgment.

The bottom front-part of the brain is the p<u>art</u> that says, "*I want.*" When you use it you have a strong desire to <u>learn</u> TO-DO creative things and invent things and discover things.

All 3-parts of the front <u>part</u> of your brain produce IMAGINATION.

This Old-World is being destroyed by The Nasty-Stuff-Family, Father-Pollution and Mother-Poverty and Sister-Sickness and Brother-War, and . . . *we must stop them before it's too late.*

THE CREATOR OF LIFE is the only one who can Create a New-World. But you, and all Children and Teenagers, will use REAL-MAGIC and IMAGINATION and the NO. 2 Pencil to create and invent and discover GOoD ways to live.

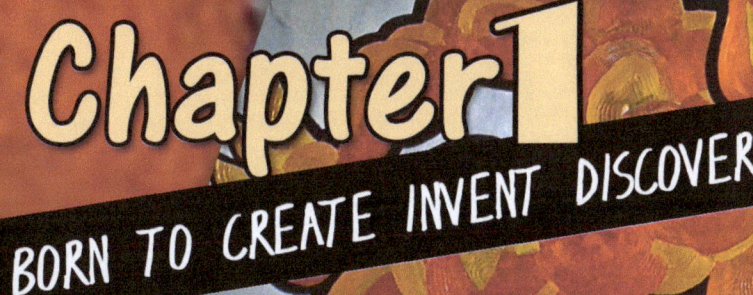

Chapter 1
I WAS BORN TO CREATE INVENT DISCOVER

–The Black-Artist John Solomon Sandridge
(Black-Boy)

My **first memory of being alive** was when I was a baby, and my gums itched and hurt.

I also remember the time when I was 2-years old. My-Mother sat me on the floor and walked away. I watched a green wiggly thing come towards me. I reached and picked it up and she *SCREAMED!* I dropped it and watched it crawl beneath the stove. I was 3-years old when I saw some strange things. My-Mother laid a quilt on the floor beside her and My-Father's bed. She put me on it so I could have a nap and left the room. I stared beneath the bed into the darkness and saw shapes.

I watched the shapes float in the air. They grew big and then small. Then grew bigger and smaller again and again. Soon the bed and the floor and the walls disappeared. The shapes turned into houses and people and planes and trees and boats and animals, and things I had Never-Ever-Seen before. This happened again and again until I was 4-years old.

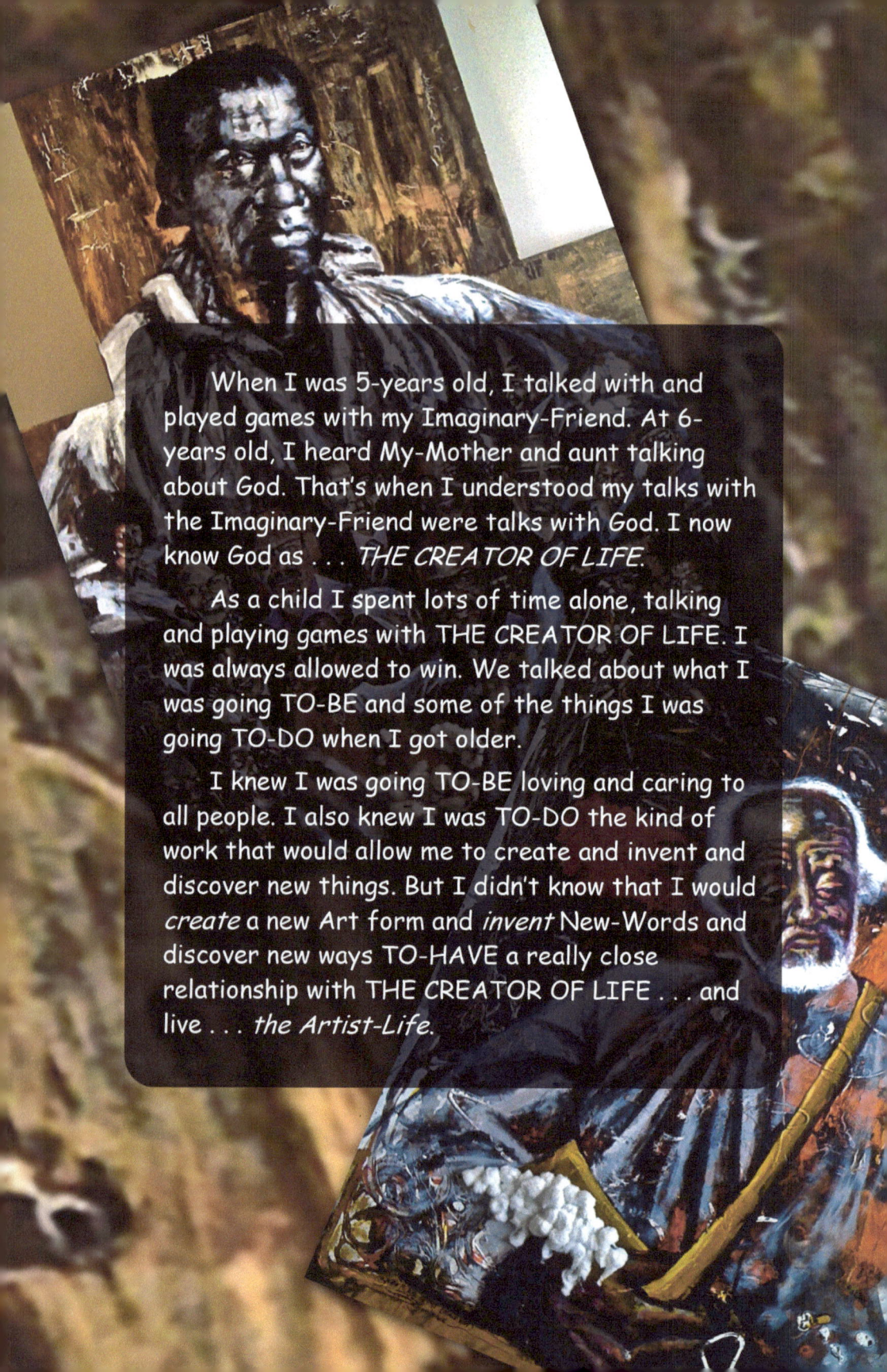

When I was 5-years old, I talked with and played games with my Imaginary-Friend. At 6-years old, I heard My-Mother and aunt talking about God. That's when I understood my talks with the Imaginary-Friend were talks with God. I now know God as . . . *THE CREATOR OF LIFE*.

As a child I spent lots of time alone, talking and playing games with THE CREATOR OF LIFE. I was always allowed to win. We talked about what I was going TO-BE and some of the things I was going TO-DO when I got older.

I knew I was going TO-BE loving and caring to all people. I also knew I was TO-DO the kind of work that would allow me to create and invent and discover new things. But I didn't know that I would *create* a new Art form and *invent* New-Words and discover new ways TO-HAVE a really close relationship with THE CREATOR OF LIFE . . . and live . . . *the Artist-Life*.

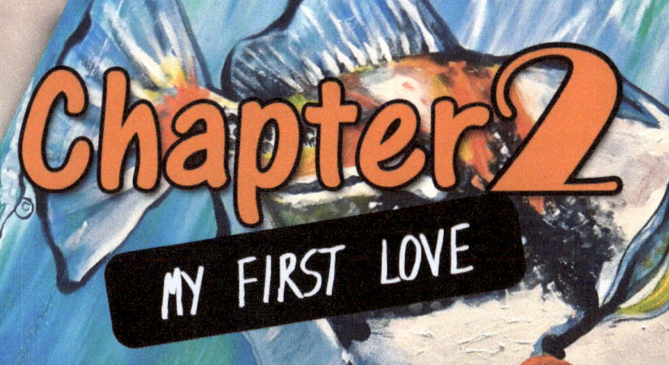

Chapter 2

MY FIRST LOVE

I was 6-years old when **I found** "my first love." It was the NO. 2 Pencil, which became a tool that was very, very *power-full**.

In grade school I <u>learned</u> to use the NO. 2 Pencil to print letters and make numbers. But that didn't make me feel happy or give me peace. Yet when I used it to draw I could feel its power, and that made me feel power-full. Then I was happy and peace-full*. That's when my Artist-Life began, and I k<u>new</u> that I was born to create and invent and discover <u>new things</u>.

One day I was alone walking in the back of my neighborhood. I saw a NO. 2 Pencil half buried in the ground and felt good seeing it. I picked it up and brushed the dirt off and smiled and put it in my pocket and went home. When I got home I took it out and smiled again and used it to draw what I enjoyed drawing most . . . *Stick-People!*

Drawing Stick-People with a NO. 2 Pencil made me feel the REAL-MAGIC that was in me. It also helped me develop my IMAGINATION and I'm-Possible attitude, and both caused my courage to grow stronger. I wanted TO-BE a real Artist and wanted TO-DO <u>good</u>* for all people.

Every day I drew Stick-People and every day, day after day, my IMAGINATION grew stronger and stronger. I was getting closer and closer to BE-ing . . . *The Black-Artist.*

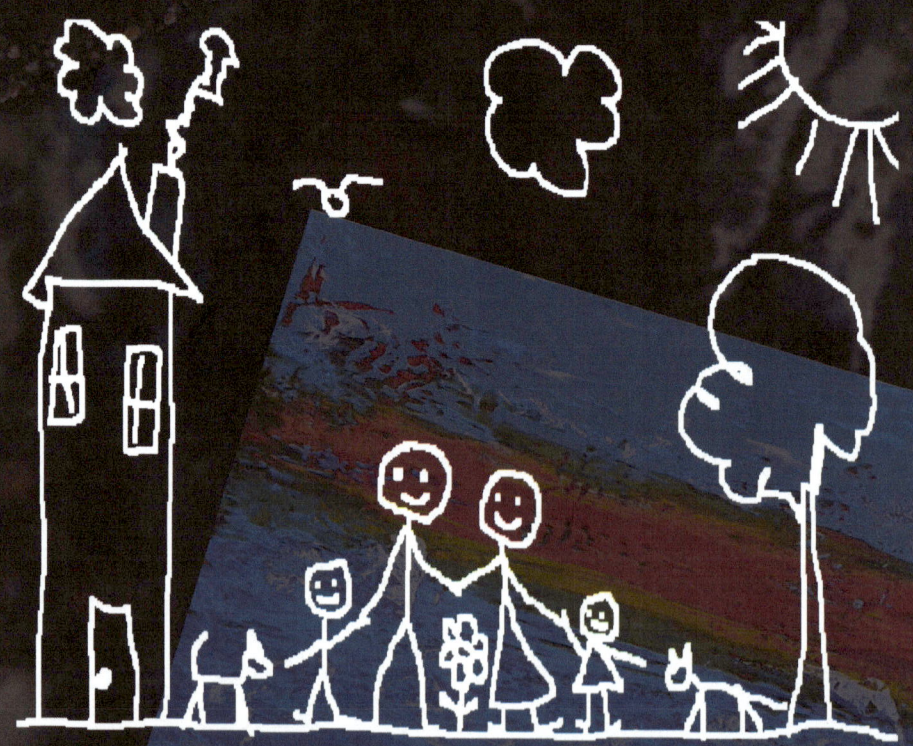

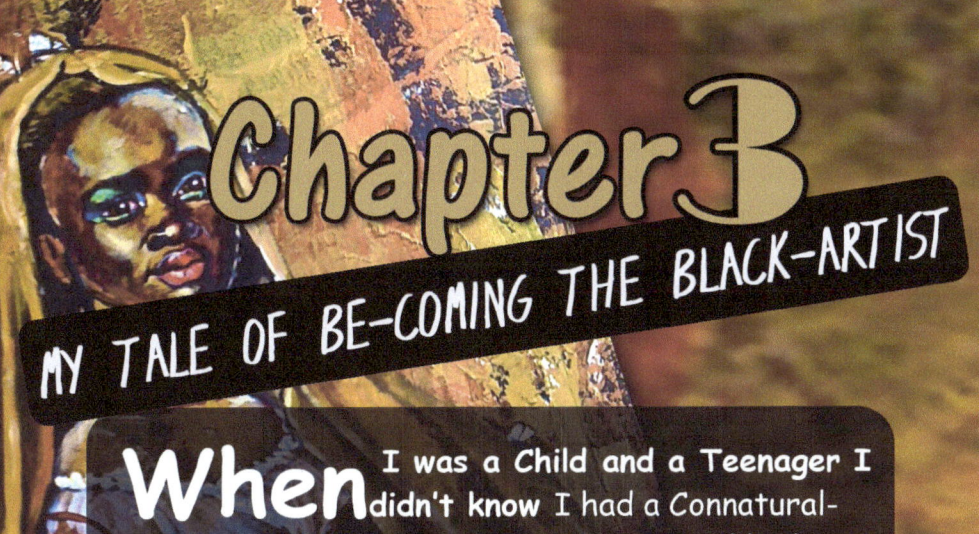

Chapter 3
MY TALE OF BE-COMING THE BLACK-ARTIST

When I was a Child and a Teenager I didn't know I had a Connatural-Desire Gland. But I knew the NO. 2 Pencil had a special *power*. I felt its power every time I saw it or held it in my hand or had it in my pocket. And when I used it to draw and write my fears and sadness and anger disappeared. But its power didn't make my shyness . . . *disappear*.

During my Childhood and Teenage years I was a loner. I was even a stranger to my own family. Most of the time I didn't go outside to play with my brothers and sisters and friends. I stayed in the house drawing because I didn't want them calling me names like dummy and stupid and fool and sissy.

The name-calling made me feel lonely and fearful and sad and very, very angry. I saw myself as a wimpy-whiny scared and mean skinny-kid. The only thing that made me feel my life could be better was the NO. 2 Pencil, and I didn't want to continue to live the way I was living.

I lived in poverty with My-Mother and My-Father and 4-Brothers and 3-Sisters. The house we lived in was a 3-room shot-gun-house. But we

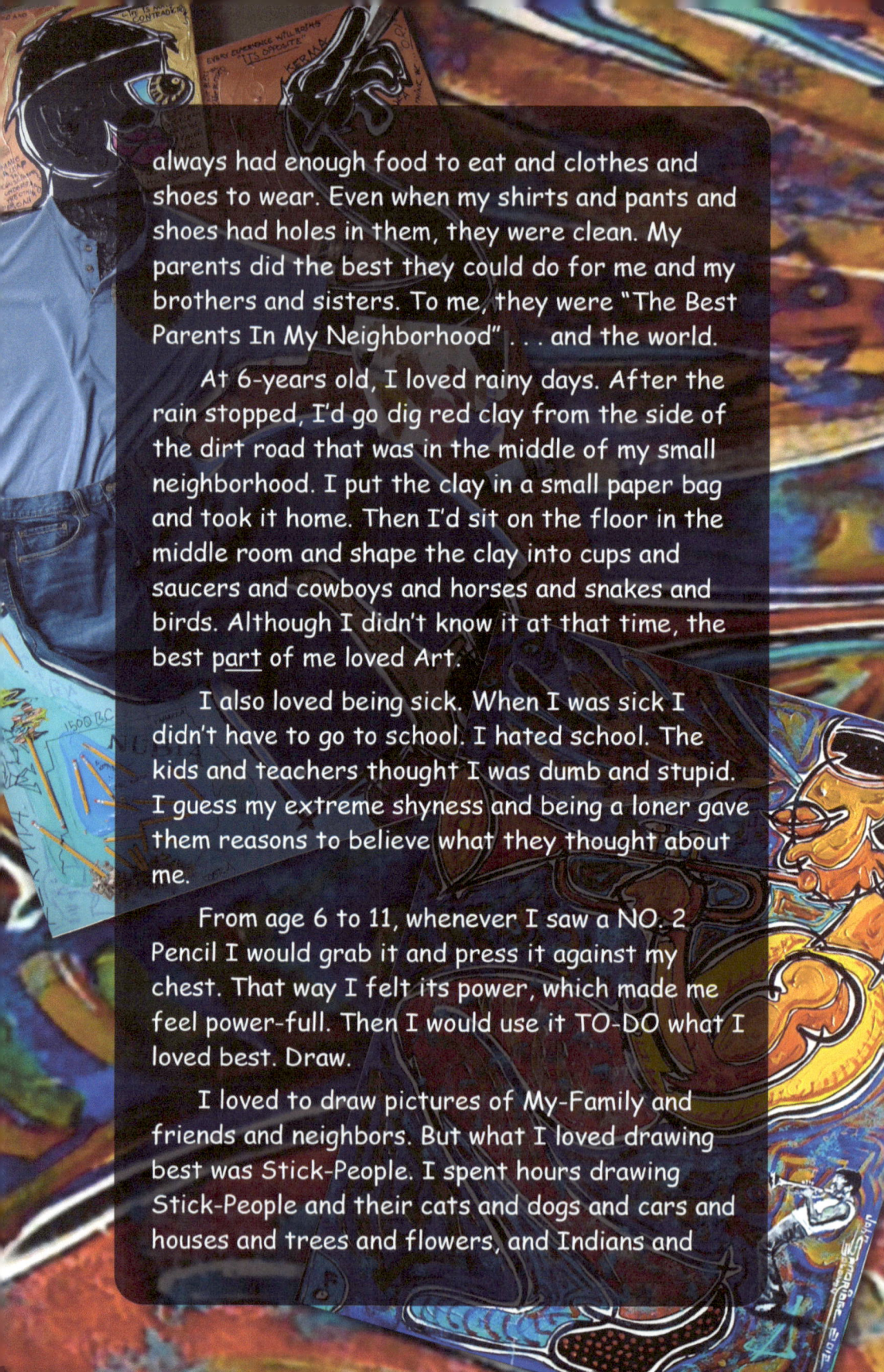

always had enough food to eat and clothes and shoes to wear. Even when my shirts and pants and shoes had holes in them, they were clean. My parents did the best they could do for me and my brothers and sisters. To me, they were "The Best Parents In My Neighborhood" . . . and the world.

At 6-years old, I loved rainy days. After the rain stopped, I'd go dig red clay from the side of the dirt road that was in the middle of my small neighborhood. I put the clay in a small paper bag and took it home. Then I'd sit on the floor in the middle room and shape the clay into cups and saucers and cowboys and horses and snakes and birds. Although I didn't know it at that time, the best <u>part</u> of me loved Art.

I also loved being sick. When I was sick I didn't have to go to school. I hated school. The kids and teachers thought I was dumb and stupid. I guess my extreme shyness and being a loner gave them reasons to believe what they thought about me.

From age 6 to 11, whenever I saw a NO. 2 Pencil I would grab it and press it against my chest. That way I felt its power, which made me feel power-full. Then I would use it TO-DO what I loved best. Draw.

I loved to draw pictures of My-Family and friends and neighbors. But what I loved drawing best was Stick-People. I spent hours drawing Stick-People and their cats and dogs and cars and houses and trees and flowers, and Indians and cowboys and jet planes and tanks and army men. After drawing them I would take a deep breath, and my sensitive-soul would rush into my chest and sit in the corner of my tender he<u>art</u>. (My-Mother always said I was tenderhe<u>arted</u>.) Then my mind would fill itself with my number 1 dream, which was a <u>Heart-Dream</u>*.

My <u>Heart-Dream</u> was TO-BE a real cartoon Artist.

I wanted to be like my favorite cartoon Artist heroes. Al Capp who created *Li'l Abner* and Charles Schulz who created *Peanuts*. I used my IMAGINATION and IMAGINATED the dream that someday I would BE a real cartoon Artist like them. That way I could BE and DO what I was created TO-BE and TO-DO. I wanted to give people reasons to feel the <u>good</u> that was in their he<u>arts</u> and laugh with their eyes.

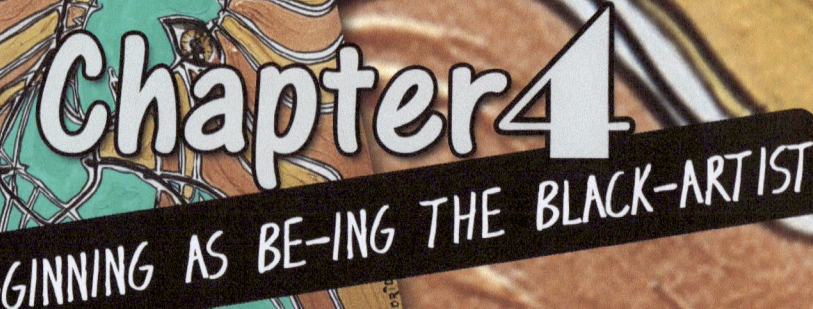

Chapter 4

MY BE-GINNING AS BE-ING THE BLACK-ARTIST

When I was a Child and Teenager there were 2-things that inspired me with the dream of wanting TO-BE a real cartoon Artist.

The cartoons I saw in my hometown newspaper, *The Gadsden Times*, were the 1ˢᵗ-thing that inspired me. The cartoons I watched on TV were the 2ⁿᵈ-thing. Both gave me a reason to BE-lieve I was going TO-BE a real cartoon Artist. But I didn't know that it would take *hard work* and lots of *patience*.

When I was 12-years old, My-Family moved from the 3-room house into a 12-room house. But my life was still the same. I stayed in the house most of the time and drew Stick-People and their world.

When I was 15-years old, my brothers and sisters began calling me *Shy-Guy*. But that didn't stop me from BE-ing a Teenager who had the I'm-Possible attitude. At that time, my Connatural-Desire Gland became strong and *pushed* me TO-DO what I needed TO-BE a real cartoon Artist.

The day came when I really was ready to make the first step. I drew 3-gag cartoons. Without getting permission from my parents, I called the local newspaper company, *The Gadsden Times News*. Before I picked up the phone to dial the number, my I'm-Possible attitude gave me a Confident-Thought. I thought, *"I'm going to sell my cartoons to* The Alabama Weekly Sunday Magazine *and be like Al Capp and Charles Schulz."*

I put a skinny finger in each hole and slowly dialed the number and waited. As I listened to the phone . . . *!RING!* . . . *!RING!* . . . *!RING!* . . . I had a *Happy-Thought*. I thought, *"I'll prove I'm a real Artist and my brothers and sisters and cousins and friends will stop calling me stupid names."* Just as I finished that thought, a White-Woman answered the phone.

She said, "Hello. This is *The Gadsden Times* newspaper."

I told her, "I want to sell my gag cartoons to the newspaper. And have them put in *The Alabama Weekly Sunday Magazine*."

The woman didn't say anything. I don't think she even moved.

All I heard was *The-Silence*. It was really !Loud!.

If you've never listened to The-Silence you're Lucky. It's dark and lonely and more frightening than *The-Loudness*. The-Loudness is bright and sparkly with purple lightning bolts at the end. Most people can *stand* The-Loudness, but there are only a few who can *sit* in The-Silence.

After awhile the woman asked me a question. She asked, "How *old* are you, son?" I was a proud Teenager who was sure that he was supposed TO-BE and Could-BE* and Would-BE* a real cartoon Artist.

I told her, "I'm 15-years old. I'm an *Artist.*"

She was quiet *again.*

The-Silence was !Louder!, and more frightening than before.

Then she said, "*Well* . . ."

And I waited.

I wanted her to say something else and she did, she spoke in a really kind voice and the words were sweet. She told me, "The gag cartoons in *The Alabama Weekly Sunday Magazine* aren't printed here. That magazine is printed in Montgomery, Alabama. You'll have to call and talk to them about . . . *your* . . . gag cartoons."

Not only was she being kind and sweet, she was BE-ing friendly and helpful. I could feel her concern in my chest, because she was trying to help me.

It was the 1960s when this happened. I was an unknown Black-Teenager living in Alabama, and I wanted to sell my untried gag cartoons to a well-known statewide magazine. That White-Woman was helping me do what I wanted TO-DO, which was to sell my cartoons and BE-come a real cartoon Artist.

As I held the big black heavy phone to my face

I had a Connatural-Desire Thought. I thought, *"If I sell my gag cartoons to this magazine, everybody in Alabama will see them and read them. I'll be like Al Capp and Charles Schulz. I'll be a real cartoonist. And I'll be the first real Artist in my family and neighborhood and school."*

As soon as that thought finished swimming through my mind, I had another thought. A Fear-Thought. It jumped into my mind and I thought, *"How do I . . . call . . . the people in Montgomery?"*

Immediately the woman asked me another question. She asked, "You got a pencil and paper, son?"

"Yes, Ma'am!" I said in a proud voice. I had a sharp NO. 2 Pencil in my pocket. It was filled with power, and I was ready to use it.

Then she told me in a kind, friendly voice, "I'll give you the number and you can call them in Montgomery. They'll tell you what you need to do to get your gag cartoons in that magazine." She called out the numbers *s / o o o w / y* and I printed them on a piece of paper I had torn from the corner of a grocery bag.

Then she said, "Don't you worry son. Everything's going to work out just fine."

My I'm-Possible attitude got stronger when I heard those words. I told her, "Thank you, Ma'am."

Next she told me something really important, and my Connatural-Desire TO-BE "The-First" Artist in my family and neighborhood and school

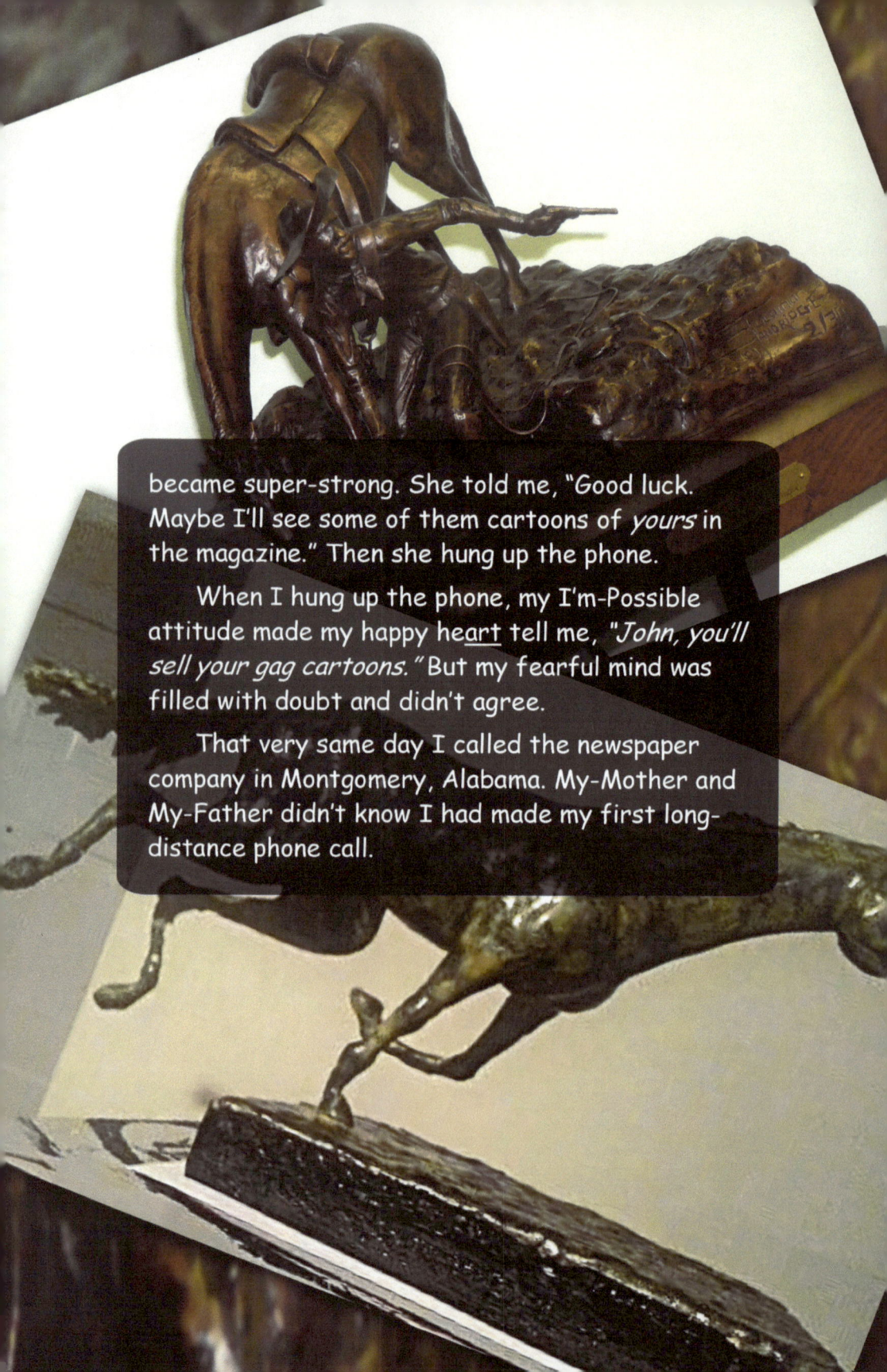

became super-strong. She told me, "Good luck. Maybe I'll see some of them cartoons of *yours* in the magazine." Then she hung up the phone.

When I hung up the phone, my I'm-Possible attitude made my happy he<u>art</u> tell me, *"John, you'll sell your gag cartoons."* But my fearful mind was filled with doubt and didn't agree.

That very same day I called the newspaper company in Montgomery, Alabama. My-Mother and My-Father didn't know I had made my first long-distance phone call.

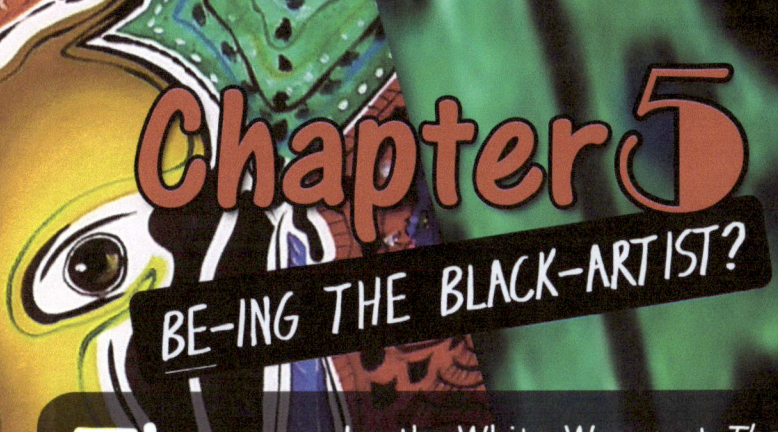

Chapter 5

BE-ING THE BLACK-ARTIST?

The same day the White-Woman at *The Gadsden Times Newspaper* gave me the phone number of *The Alabama Weekly Sunday Magazine*, I called it. I listened to the loud . . . !RING! . . !RING! . . !RING! . . . that jumped through the phone and into my ear. I waited. My fearful mind filled itself with The-Silence and then The-Loudness.

I sat there and held the phone to my ear, waiting. The-Loudness and The-Silence filled my mind with fear and *sticky-thoughts* that made my hand and arm shake. I waited for someone to answer my call. My mind thought about what my mouth was going to say. The phone was becoming heavier. Before my mind could come up with what I would say, a White-Woman said, "Hello, this is *The Alabama Weekly Sunday Magazine*."

I jumped!

I looked around the room, and squeezed my NO. 2 Pencil. Its power calmed me down. Then I told the woman, "I'm an *Artist* and I want to get my gag cartoons put in *The Alabama Weekly Sunday Magazine*."

The-Silence came back and **swelled**. It grew !Louder! and bounced sideways in and out of my ears.

Then she asked me a question. She asked, "How . . . *old* . . . are you?"

"I'm 15-years old," I told her with pride.

"You're . . . *15-years old?*"

"Yes Ma'am," I told her with more pride. I had already drawn 3-gag cartoons and added the words to them. So I felt I was ready TO-BE a real cartoon Artist.

In a *fast* and *strong* voice the woman told me, "What you need to do is send the drawings and the words to the magazine here in Montgomery. *If* . . . they . . . *like* . . . them . . . you'll get 5-dollars for the ones accepted."

Boy I felt really good, and was on top of the world dancing the Boo-Ga-Lu. With strong pride I told the woman, "Thank you, thank you." But what she said next was a big surprise.

In a kind voice she said, "Good luck." And her words sounded like she was smiling and was happy for me. I hung up the phone and grinned until my cheeks were tight and sore. I was on my way to BE-ing a real cartoon Artist.

After talking with the woman at *The Alabama Weekly Sunday Magazine*, 1-week passed. The following Sunday I sat in my Safe-Place, the bedroom, with my only friends— the drawing board and a NO. 2 Pencil. I drew another gag cartoon and added words. I thought I was ready TO-BE a cartoon Artist just like Al Capp and Charles Schulz, who truly were real cartoon Artists.

Without my parents knowing what I was doing, I put the 4-gag cartoons in an envelope and mailed them to *The Alabama Weekly Sunday Magazine* in Montgomery. I waited for 2-days and got no response. After 1-week passed, I still hadn't received a response. I felt sad and hopeless. I was a 15-year-old failure.

After 2-weeks passed, I had a Fear-Thought. I thought, *"I can't be a real cartoon Artist. I'm what my brothers and sisters and friends call me. I'm stupid for thinking I can be a real cartoon Artist like Al Capp and Charles Schulz. I am dumb . . . and . . . I'm a black fool!"*

I really wanted TO-BE a real cartoon Artist more than anything. But I felt I wasn't one because things weren't happening as fast as I thought they should. So I gave up on the idea about BE-ing a real cartoon Artist. I also forgot about the 4-gag cartoons I had sent to *The Alabama Weekly Sunday Magazine.*

But, there was a question.

The question was, did I really, really, really have an *I'm-Possible* attitude and was my *Connatural-Desire Gland* strong enough to push me to be "The-First" cartoon Artist in my family and neighborhood and school?

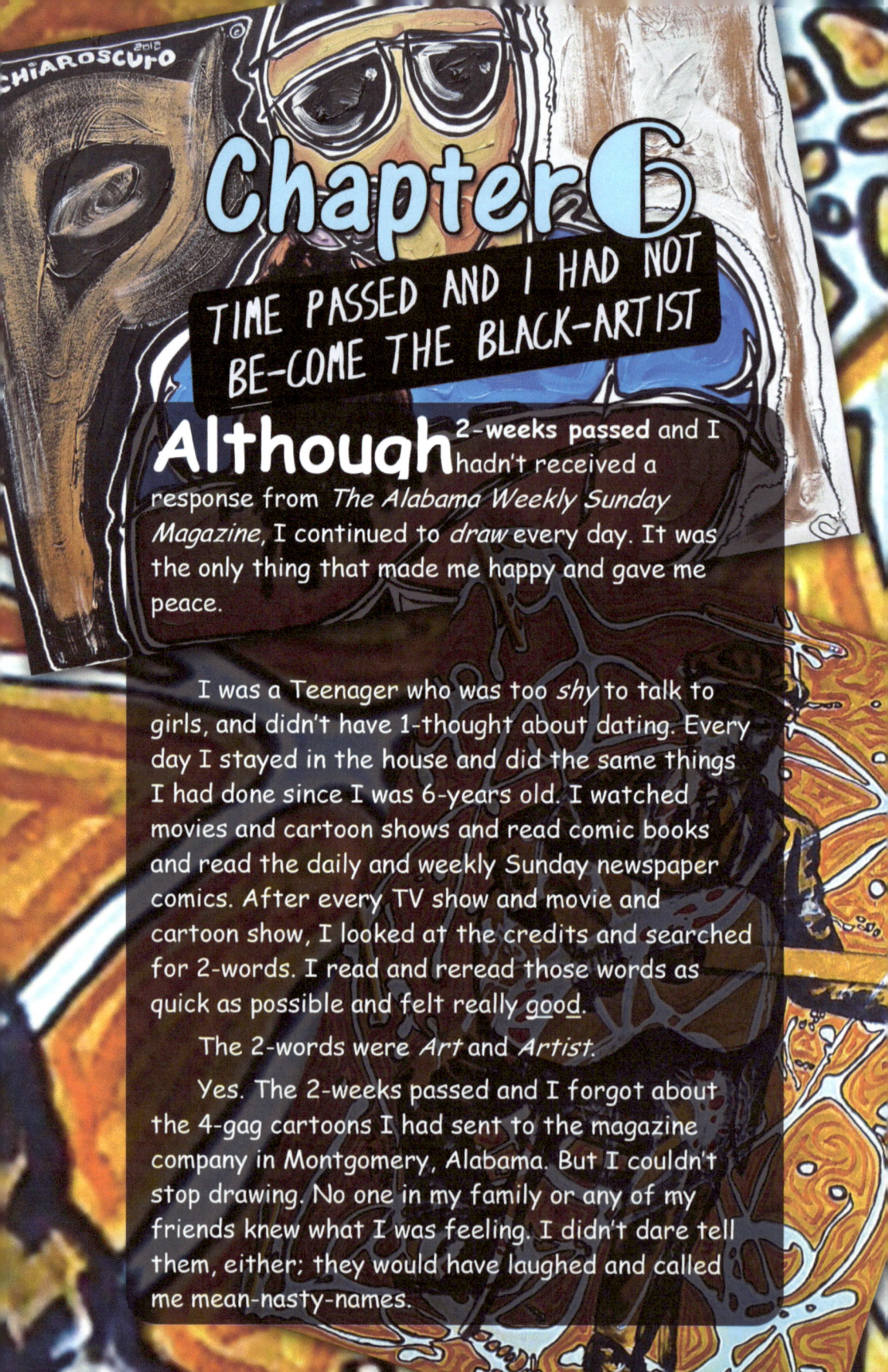

Chapter 6

TIME PASSED AND I HAD NOT BE-COME THE BLACK-ARTIST

Although 2-weeks passed and I hadn't received a response from *The Alabama Weekly Sunday Magazine*, I continued to *draw* every day. It was the only thing that made me happy and gave me peace.

I was a Teenager who was too *shy* to talk to girls, and didn't have 1-thought about dating. Every day I stayed in the house and did the same things I had done since I was 6-years old. I watched movies and cartoon shows and read comic books and read the daily and weekly Sunday newspaper comics. After every TV show and movie and cartoon show, I looked at the credits and searched for 2-words. I read and reread those words as quick as possible and felt really <u>good</u>.

The 2-words were *Art* and *Artist*.

Yes. The 2-weeks passed and I forgot about the 4-gag cartoons I had sent to the magazine company in Montgomery, Alabama. But I couldn't stop drawing. No one in my family or any of my friends knew what I was feeling. I didn't dare tell them, either; they would have laughed and called me mean-nasty-names.

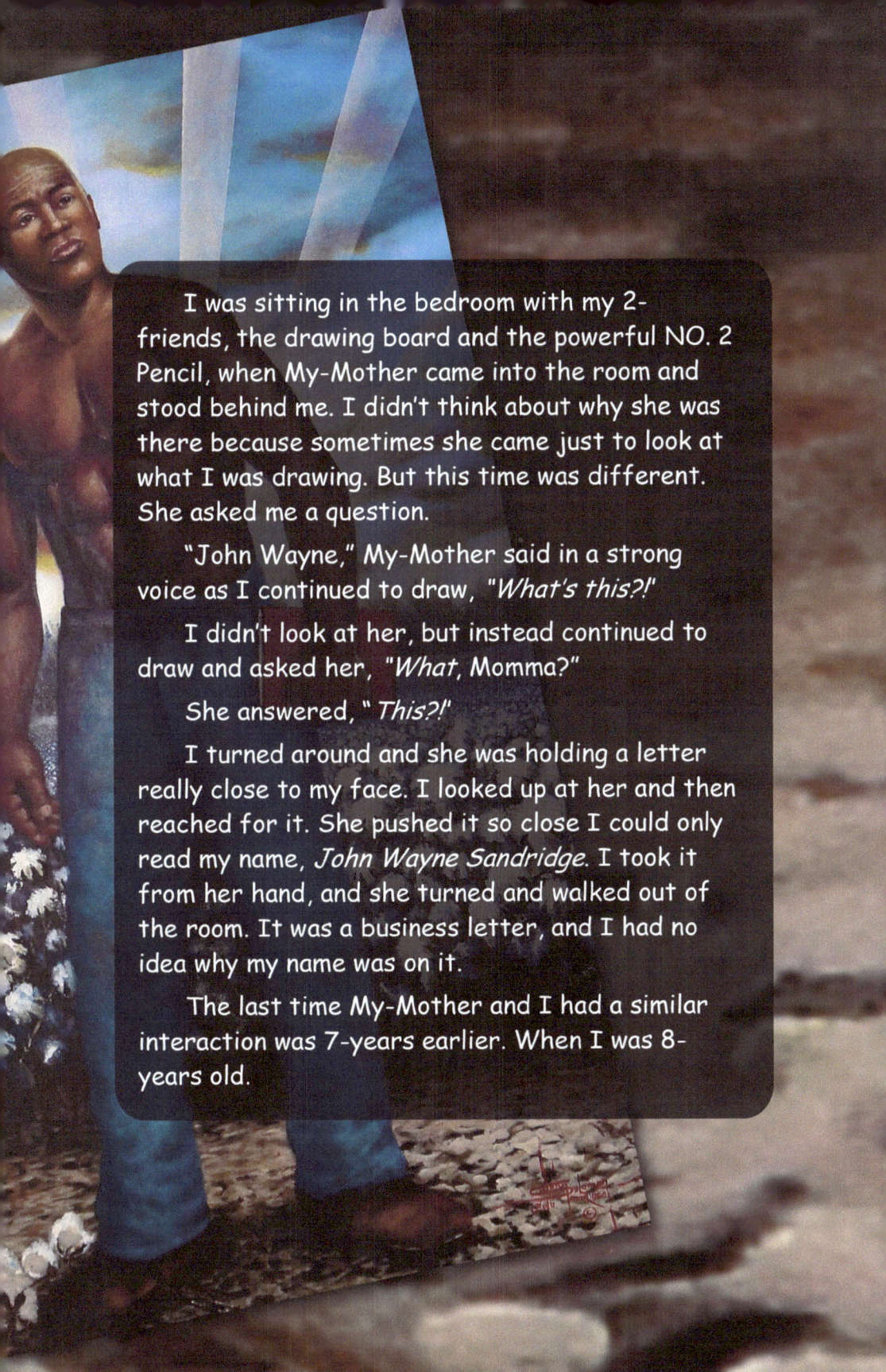

I was sitting in the bedroom with my 2-friends, the drawing board and the powerful NO. 2 Pencil, when My-Mother came into the room and stood behind me. I didn't think about why she was there because sometimes she came just to look at what I was drawing. But this time was different. She asked me a question.

"John Wayne," My-Mother said in a strong voice as I continued to draw, *"What's this?!"*

I didn't look at her, but instead continued to draw and asked her, *"What,* Momma?"

She answered, *"This?!"*

I turned around and she was holding a letter really close to my face. I looked up at her and then reached for it. She pushed it so close I could only read my name, *John Wayne Sandridge.* I took it from her hand, and she turned and walked out of the room. It was a business letter, and I had no idea why my name was on it.

The last time My-Mother and I had a similar interaction was 7-years earlier. When I was 8-years old.

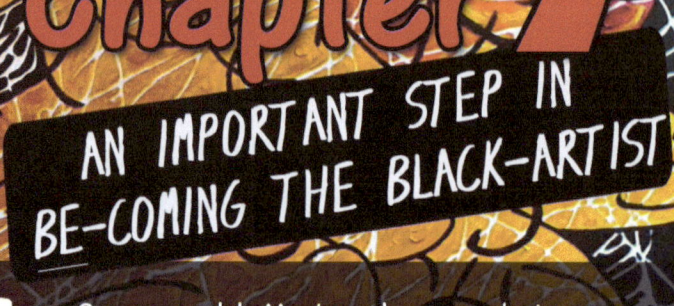

Chapter 7

AN IMPORTANT STEP IN BE-COMING THE BLACK-ARTIST

I was 8-years old. My brothers and sisters were outside playing with kids in the neighborhood. I was doing another thing I loved, sitting at the kitchen table eating cornflakes and reading from the cereal box. That day my Connatural-Desire Gland pushed me TO-DO something no one in my family had Never-Ever-Done before. Not even My-Father or My-Mother, and that made me BE . . . *"The-First."*

I read the front and both sides of the cereal box. Then I turned the box around to read the backside and look at the pictures. The picture on the back was a *toy submarine.* I read the words *IT'S JUST LIKE THE REAL THING! IT FLOATS. IT DIVES. AND IT RESURFACES! JUST ADD BAKING SODA AND PUT IT IN WATER!* After reading those words I had a *WOW!-* Thought. I thought, *"WOW! I gotta get me one of them."* I hurried and ate the last bite of soggy cornflakes.

I got up from the table and ran into the front room of our 3-room house, which was the living room. My-Mother's sister slept on the green couch in the front room. At the end of the couch was a small table where she kept envelopes and stamps and notebook paper. I took an envelope, but there were no stamps. I ran into the middle room where my 4-bothers and 3-sisters and I slept. I used a butter knife to get a quarter out of my piggybank. I loved saving money and giving it to others almost as much as I loved drawing Stick-People.

After I had gotten the quarter from the piggybank, I ran to the back room, the kitchen. That's where My-Mother and My-Father slept on a really *small* bed. I sat at the table and tore the label from the top of the cornflakes box and printed the words John Wayne Sandridge, 624 Lister Lane, Gadsden, Alabama on it. Then I printed the same thing and the company's address on the envelope and put the label and quarter inside, and sealed it.

Later that day I went downtown with my older brother. After we had walked a short distance I told him something that made him really mad. I told him, "I need to go to the post office."

He looked at me and yelled, "*For what?!*"

I looked at him with my angriest eyes and yelled, "*I need to do something!*"

He stared at me and screamed as loud as he could, "*JOHN WAYNE DO SOMETHING STUPID AND WE'LL GET IN TROUBLE!!!!*"

I screamed, "*I KNOW! AND I AIN'T STUPID!!!!!*"

He stared at me.

I stared at him.

We were *2-really-angry-brothers*.

Eventually we went into the Post Office staring Anger-Thoughts at each other. When he turned away I quickly went to the counter and bought a stamp and licked the back of it and put it on the envelope and shoved it back into my pocket. Then I walked slowly over to him and asked a question. I asked him, "Where do I put my letter?"

He looked at me and with all of his anger, yelled a really quiet scream, *"WHAT LETTER?!!!!"*

I took the letter from my pocket and held it up and yelled a quiet scream, *"THIS LETTER!!!!!"*

He leaned close to me and whispered a yell, *"Where'd you get that letter from, boy?!"*

I held the letter behind me and stepped backwards and yelled, *"This is my letter! And you're not getting it!"*

He looked around the post office and frowned. With all of his worst anger, he pointed a finger at a slot in the wall. I looked at his finger and then at the slot. I smiled and rushed over and shoved the letter in until it was completely out of sight.

While we walked home he was angry and didn't say a word. And I didn't care.

For 2-days I checked the mailbox hoping my toy submarine had come. Then 1-week passed and 2-weeks passed. I forgot about the idea of sitting in the bathtub filled with warm water and playing with it.

At the end of the 2nd-week, My-Mother came into the middle room where I was drawing. For the first time she asked a question I couldn't answer. She asked, "What's *this*?" When I heard her voice I jumped, and was surprised to see her standing behind me. I leaned back and looked up at her. She was holding something in her hand, and it was so close to my face I couldn't see what it was.

She asked again, "What is this, boy?"

"I don't know," I told her and slowly turned to my drawing again.

"Why's *your name* on it?" She asked me.

I turned again and looked. She was holding a small brown box close to my face. I moved back, and I saw my name on it. I felt good inside. Then I had an Exciting-Thought. I thought, *"It's my toy submarine!"*

I looked into My-Mother's eyes and smiled. She pushed the box at me, and I took it from her hand and tore it open as she watched. Inside was the toy submarine. I took it out and held it up for her to see.

She asked me, "What's *that*?"

"It's the submarine I ordered from the cornflakes box."

"Where did you get the *money* from?"

I looked up at her and said, "I got it out of . . . Frankie."

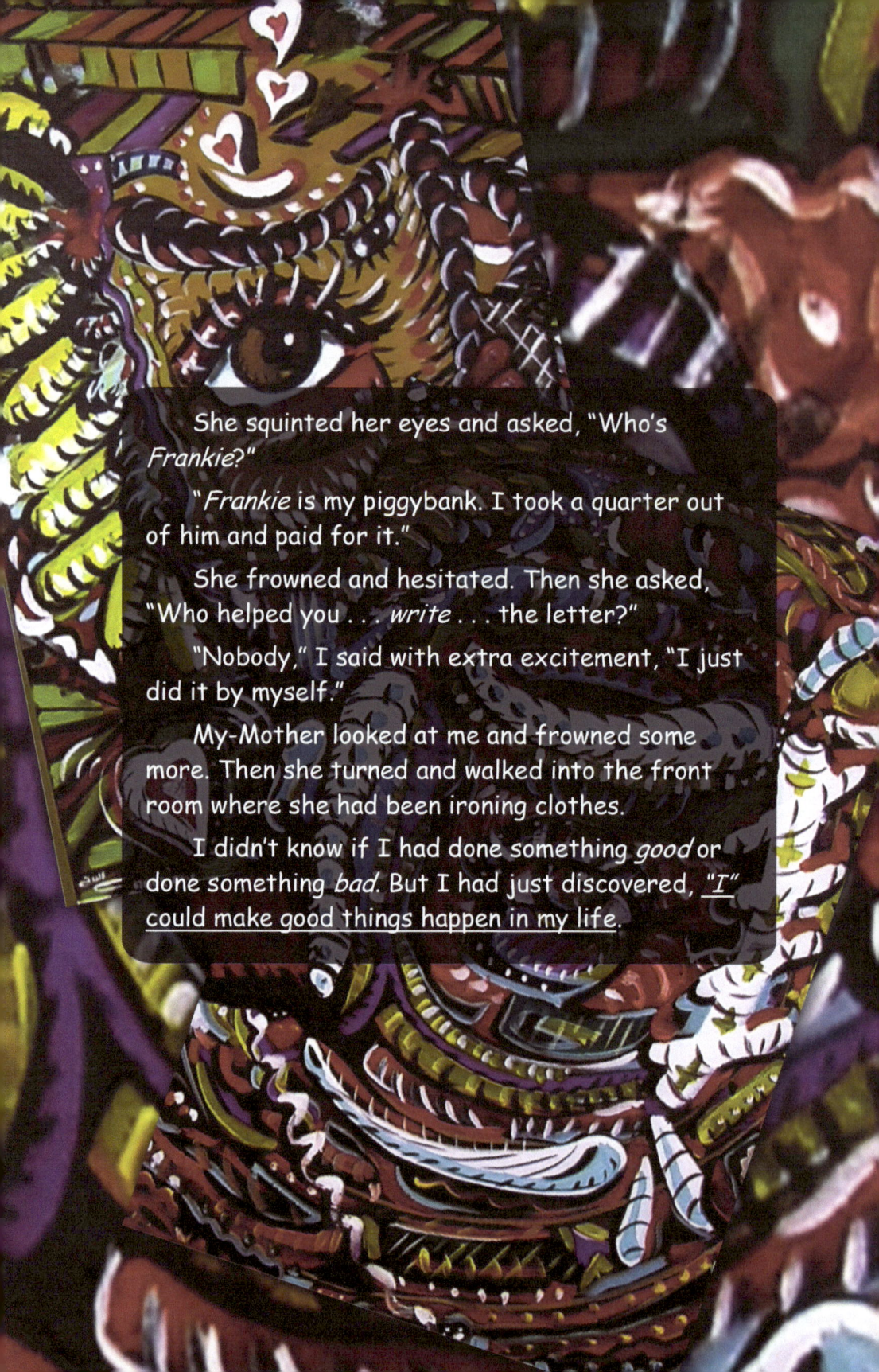

She squinted her eyes and asked, "Who's *Frankie*?"

"*Frankie* is my piggybank. I took a quarter out of him and paid for it."

She frowned and hesitated. Then she asked, "Who helped you . . . *write* . . . the letter?"

"Nobody," I said with extra excitement, "I just did it by myself."

My-Mother looked at me and frowned some more. Then she turned and walked into the front room where she had been ironing clothes.

I didn't know if I had done something *good* or done something *bad*. But I had just discovered, <u>*"I"*</u> <u>could make good things happen in my life.</u>

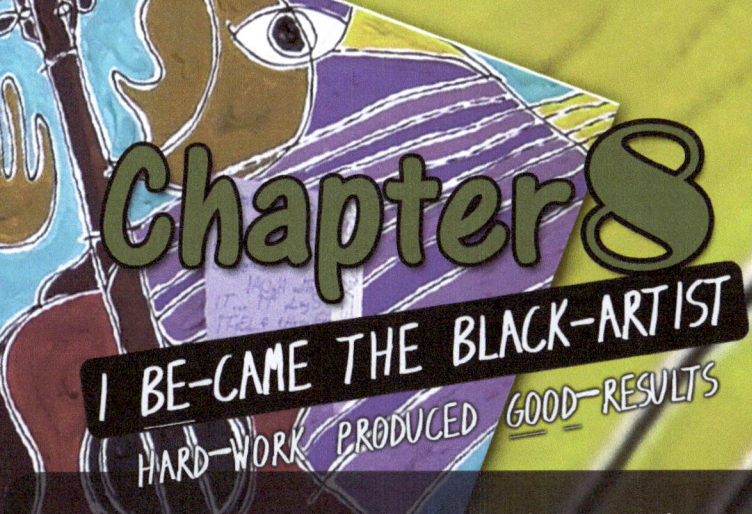

Chapter 8

I BE-CAME THE BLACK-ARTIST

HARD-WORK PRODUCED GOOD-RESULTS

Now I'll get back to the business letter I received when I was 15-years old. It was a Saturday morning and My-Family and I were living in the 12-room house. My-Mother had come into the bedroom where I was drawing. She held the letter so close to my face that I could only read my name, and I had no idea why it was on a business letter. She handed it to me and left the room before I could open it. I held it and stared *only* at my name.

That was the second time I saw my name on a letter and felt good about BE-ing me. Also whenever I heard someone say my name, *"John Wayne,"* there was something inside of me that let me know . . . *I was real.*

I tore the letter open and looked inside, and was really surprised and shocked. I reached in and pulled the paper out. I held it above my head and smiled a happy-face smile.

My smile grew and **grew** and **grew** until it was wider than my face. What I held in my hand was a check. *The-Check.* "The-First" check I

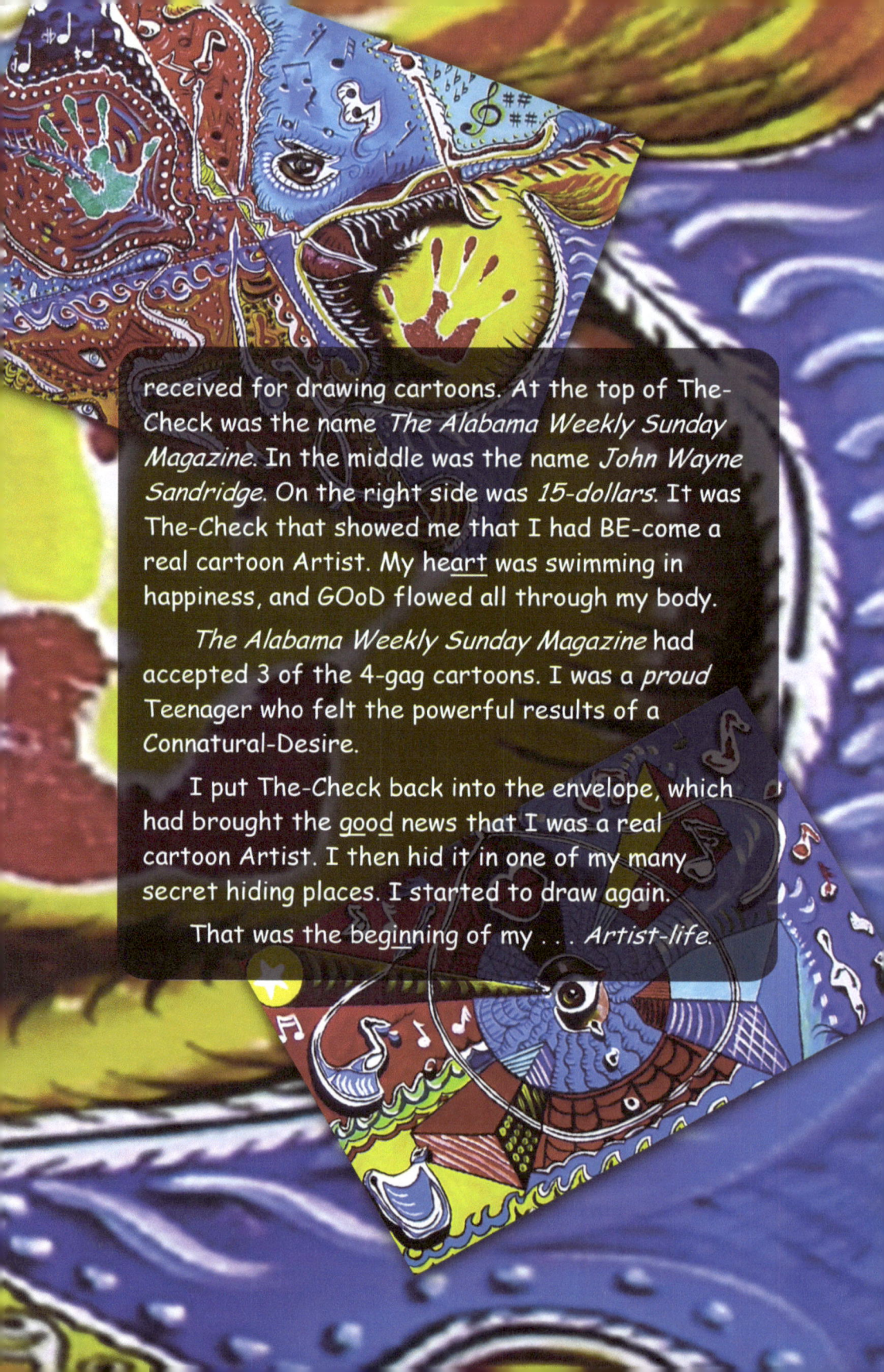

received for drawing cartoons. At the top of The-Check was the name *The Alabama Weekly Sunday Magazine*. In the middle was the name *John Wayne Sandridge*. On the right side was *15-dollars*. It was The-Check that showed me that I had BE-come a real cartoon Artist. My he<u>art</u> was swimming in happiness, and GOoD flowed all through my body.

 The Alabama Weekly Sunday Magazine had accepted 3 of the 4-gag cartoons. I was a *proud* Teenager who felt the powerful results of a Connatural-Desire.

 I put The-Check back into the envelope, which had brought the <u>good</u> news that I was a real cartoon Artist. I then hid it in one of my many secret hiding places. I started to draw again.

 That was the beg<u>inn</u>ing of my . . . *Artist-life*.

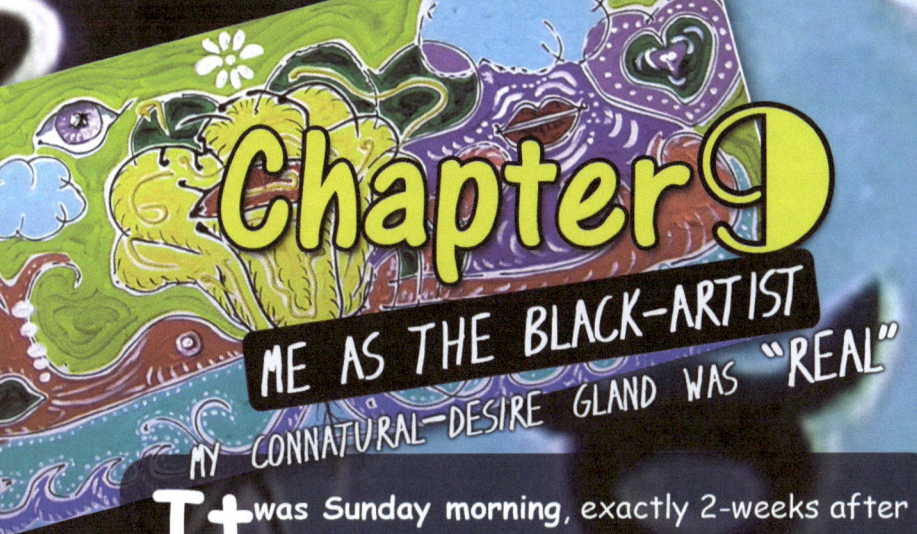

Chapter 9

ME AS THE BLACK-ARTIST
MY CONNATURAL-DESIRE GLAND WAS "REAL"

It was **Sunday morning**, exactly 2-weeks after I had received The-Check. I was sitting in the bedroom DO-ing what I loved most. Drawing.

Although The-Check was proof that I was a real cartoon Artist, that Sunday morning I was feeling sad and angry. My-Mother had yelled at me. She called me bad-names. I only got angry when my brothers and sisters and the kids in the neighborhood called me bad-names. Their favorite name for me was *"House Cat."*

But when My-Mother called me a <u>certain name</u>, I'd cry like a little baby.

Most Sunday mornings my brothers and sisters and I sat at our parent's bedroom door. We waited there for our Father to finish reading the paper and the Sunday Comic Strips. Afterwards he gave the comics paper to whoever was first in line. Most times I was first because my brothers and sisters liked sleeping late on Sundays. But since I was sad and angry that Sunday morning I waited in my bedroom, and no one was at my parent's bedroom door. I heard their door open but continued TO-DO what I was DO-ing. Drawing.

Before I could turn around, My-Father had walked into the room and was standing behind me. I leaned back and looked up at him. He was looking down at me and his eyes were really serious. He was holding something. My he<u>art</u> felt scared and my legs wanted to run, but I kept them calm. I looked down at his hand and saw *The Alabama Weekly Sunday Magazine.* He looked at the magazine and turned to a certain page. He held it up in front of me. I looked at him and *slooooowly* leaned forward. I *staaaaared* at the page. Then I looked up into his eyes. He was looking down into mine. I looked at the page again. My he<u>art</u> filled itself and my body with warm, warm, warm love.

I looked up at My-Father again. His smile had left his lips and gone up into his eyes. I don't remember whose smile was the *biggest* and *brightest.* But I remember we were smiling together and I liked it more than most things. All but . . . *drawing.*

He handed the magazine to me and turned and walked out of the room. I held it closer and stared at "The-First" gag cartoon I had published in the statewide magazine. I felt like I had BE-come a real cartoon A-R-T-I-S-T.

I don't remember if My-Family was happy because of what I had done. But I think they were.

I went to my secret hiding place and got The-Check and hugged it. Then I hugged *The Alabama Sunday Weekly Magazine* and The-Check to my chest.

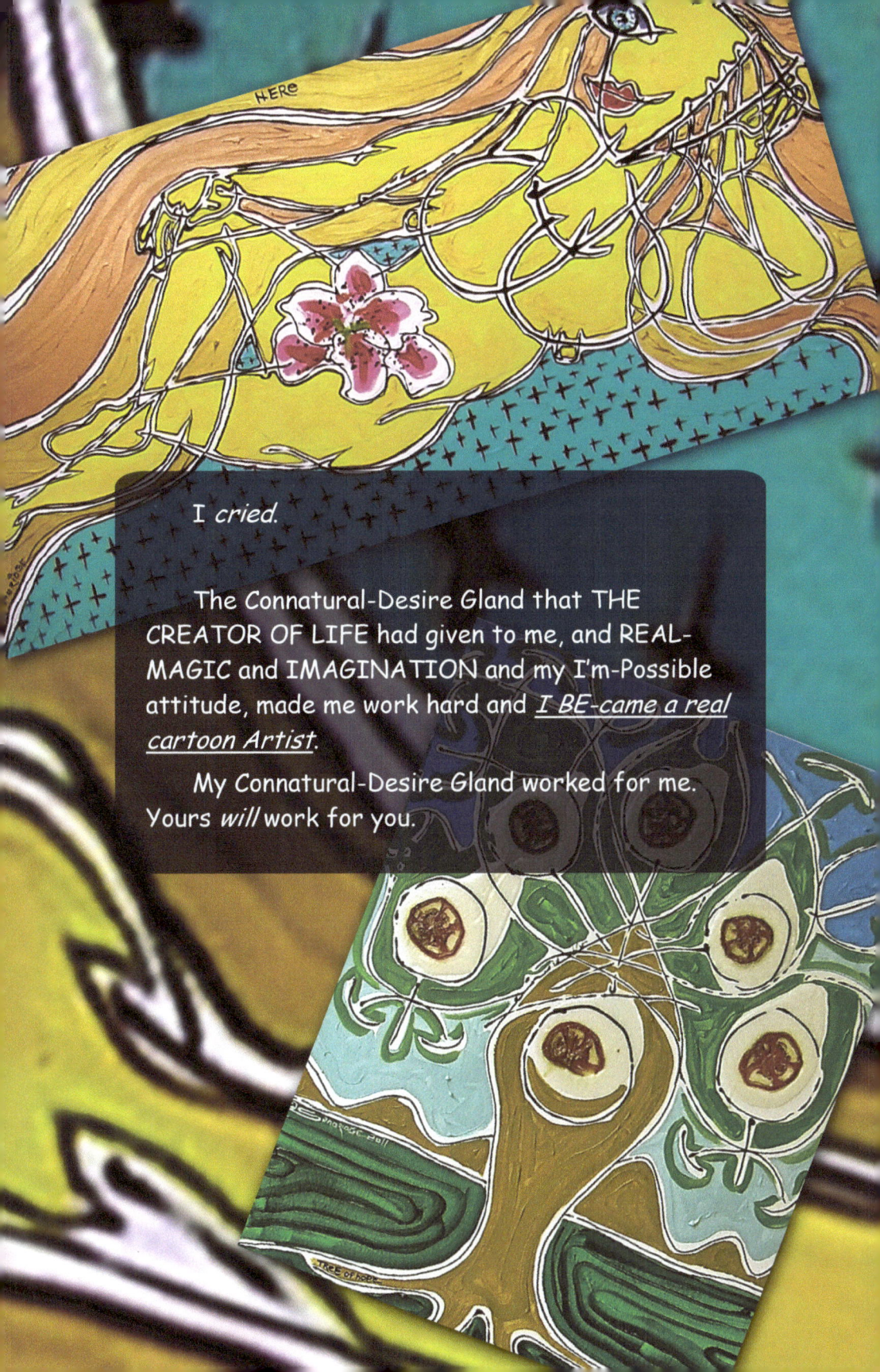

I *cried*.

The Connatural-Desire Gland that THE CREATOR OF LIFE had given to me, and REAL-MAGIC and IMAGINATION and my I'm-Possible attitude, made me work hard and *I BE-came a real cartoon Artist*.

My Connatural-Desire Gland worked for me. Yours *will* work for you.

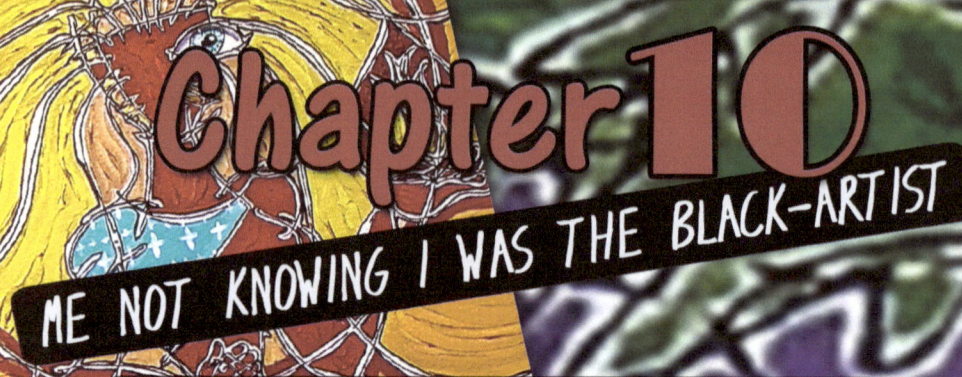

Chapter 10

ME NOT KNOWING I WAS THE BLACK-ARTIST

Did you see it? See how my Connatural-Desire Gland worked when I was 8-years old? It *pushed* me to order the toy submarine without needing help. When I was 15-years old it pushed me to know how to sell 3-gag cartoons by myself. I was BE-ing and DO-ing what THE CREATOR OF LIFE Created me TO-BE and TO-DO. I was a real cartoon Artist. *Buuuut* . . . it didn't last.

At 16-years old I met an Artist friend. He told me he was taking Art lessons from an older guy who was home from college. My new friend liked my sister and wanted to talk to her. I wanted to use his paints and brushes. So I made a *deal* with him. I told him I would ask my sister to talk to him if he would loan me his oil paints and brushes and give me 2-canvas boards.

And . . . he did.

Since I had never painted before, my 1st-painting was a *mess*. The 2nd-painting was okay, and I wanted to paint another picture. But I didn't have any canvas boards or money to buy more.

I felt good about the 2nd-painting and had a Connatural-Desire Thought. I thought, *"I'll make*

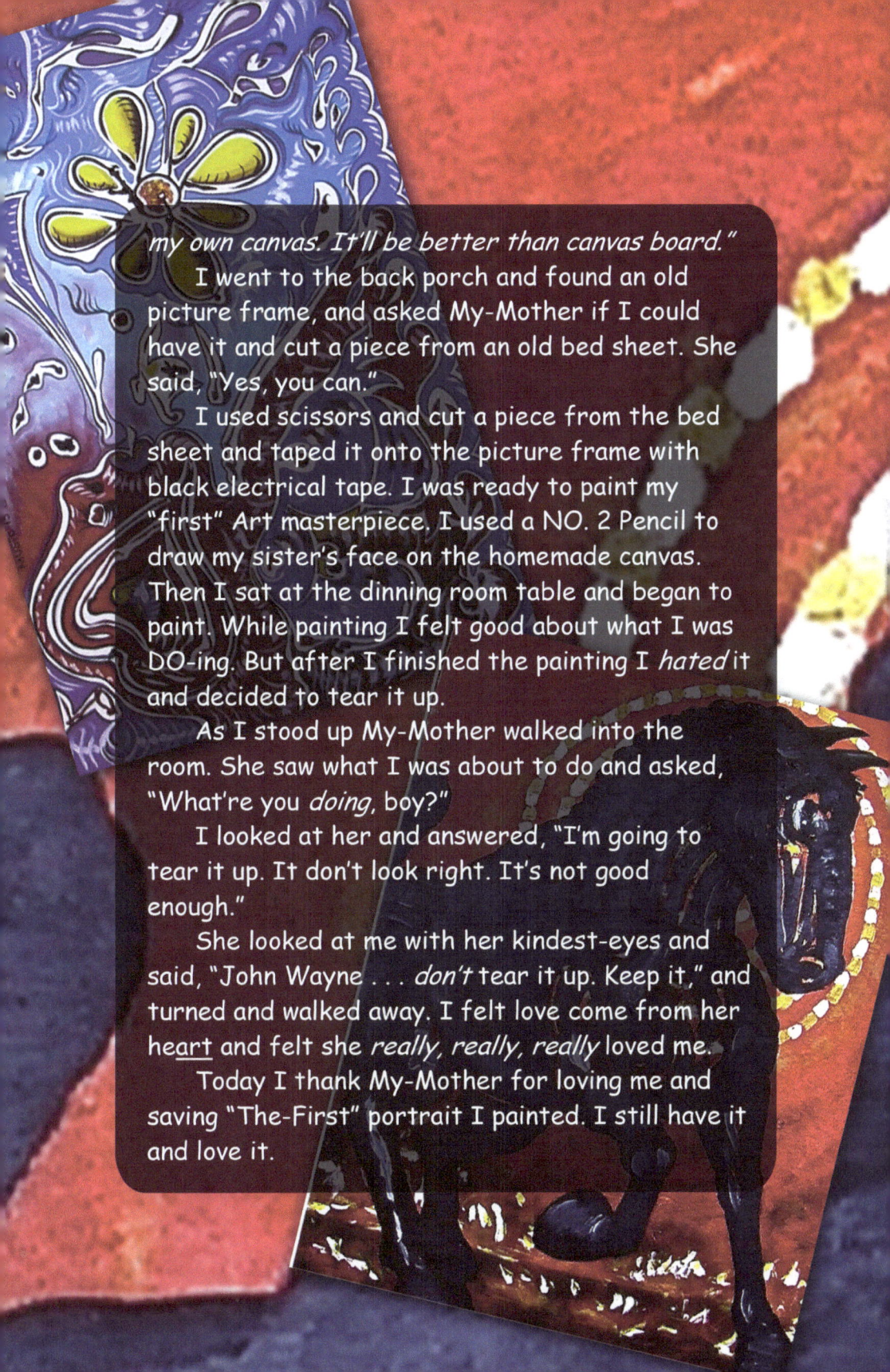

my own canvas. It'll be better than canvas board."

I went to the back porch and found an old picture frame, and asked My-Mother if I could have it and cut a piece from an old bed sheet. She said, "Yes, you can."

I used scissors and cut a piece from the bed sheet and taped it onto the picture frame with black electrical tape. I was ready to paint my "first" Art masterpiece. I used a NO. 2 Pencil to draw my sister's face on the homemade canvas. Then I sat at the dinning room table and began to paint. While painting I felt good about what I was DO-ing. But after I finished the painting I *hated* it and decided to tear it up.

As I stood up My-Mother walked into the room. She saw what I was about to do and asked, "What're you *doing*, boy?"

I looked at her and answered, "I'm going to tear it up. It don't look right. It's not good enough."

She looked at me with her kindest-eyes and said, "John Wayne . . . *don't* tear it up. Keep it," and turned and walked away. I felt love come from her he<u>art</u> and felt she *really, really, really* loved me.

Today I thank My-Mother for loving me and saving "The-First" portrait I painted. I still have it and love it.

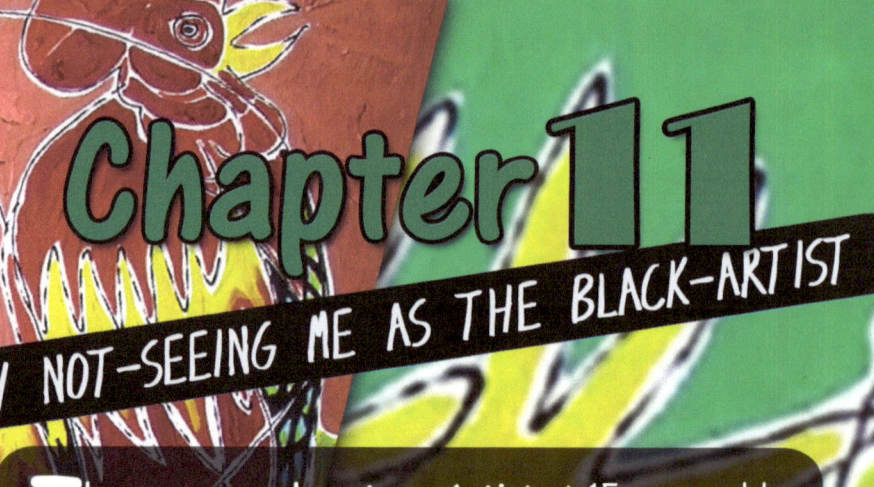

Chapter 11

MY NOT-SEEING ME AS THE BLACK-ARTIST

I **became a real cartoon Artist** at 15-years old. When I was 16-years old I met my new Artist friend and became a painter. Drawing and painting were still fun, but not like before. I had been called sissy-boy long enough and was ready for a change. My Connatural-Desire Gland was *pushing* me again, and I meet another friend and found . . . *a new love.*

My other new friend had 3-friends, and they had a musical rock band. He played lead and bass guitar. Just like my Artist friend, he liked my sister and wanted to talk to her. So I made another *deal.* He taught me to play the guitar, and I asked my sister if she would talk to him.

She did.

After I learned to play the guitar, I taught My-Father and a brother and that same sister to play too. I loved it so much I practiced *every day.* My-Father saw how much I loved it and how good I had become, and one day he came home with a used guitar. He gave it to me and I was in heaven. Then I had a really strong Connatural-Desire Thought. I thought, *"I'm going to start a rock-and-roll band. We'll travel and perform and people will like our*

COCK of the ROOST

music."

I wanted TO-HAVE a rock-and-roll band so much that I practiced every day for 1-year. When I was 17-years old I formed a band. I started with a 3-player band. I played lead guitar and a friend played bass guitar and another friend played drums. We practiced every day. Soon I had 13-players in my band. There were 7-instruments and 2-boy singers and 4-girl singers. We named it *The Soulful Soul-Brothers* and traveled and performed in Alabama and Georgia. The people loved our music. Sometimes they thought we were The Jackson 5, and asked for our autographs. I loved it.

For me there were 3-really bad things about performing and traveling and making music. I started smoking cigarettes and drinking alcohol and taking drugs. I was killing my body and mind. *Dahhhhhh*, and didn't know it!

At 23-years old I understood my addiction was killing me, and I was ready to stop. My band broke-up and I stopped the addiction. I started *searching* for THE CREATOR OF LIFE, who was not lost, although I was. I started BE-living* *in* and talking *with* THE CREATOR OF LIFE *again*, the same as I did when I was a child.

My Connatural-Desire Gland grew stronger and clearer.

Soon I started my own sign-painting business. I painted signs and wall murals throughout my hometown. My Connatural-Desire Gland continued to grow and get stronger, and I had another

Connatural-Desire Thought. I thought, *"I want to close my sign-painting business and start teaching art classes."*

I did.

I closed my sign business and opened my "first" Art studio and gallery, which was "The-First" large studio and gallery in the city. I named it, *SANDRIDGE ART STUDIO AND GALLERIES*. I taught Art classes to Children and Teenagers and . . . *Adults*.

Then one day I got a call from the superintendent of The Gadsden City School System. He wanted to talk to me. I met with him at his office, and he asked me a question. He asked, "John, will you be a member of an Art team and help create an Art program for the city school system?"

I said, "Yes, sir."

So I worked with a musician and a writer who also had talked with the superintendent. Together we created *The Gadsden City School Arts Program*.

Later I got another call from the superintendent. I met with him and he asked me another question. He asked, "John, will you teach Art in the city's schools from grades 1 through 12?"

"Yes sir, I will." I told him. I taught Art in the schools and continued to teach private lessons in my Art studio and gallery.

Then I got another call. The superintendent wanted to talk with me *again*. He wanted me to become the director of The Gadsden City School

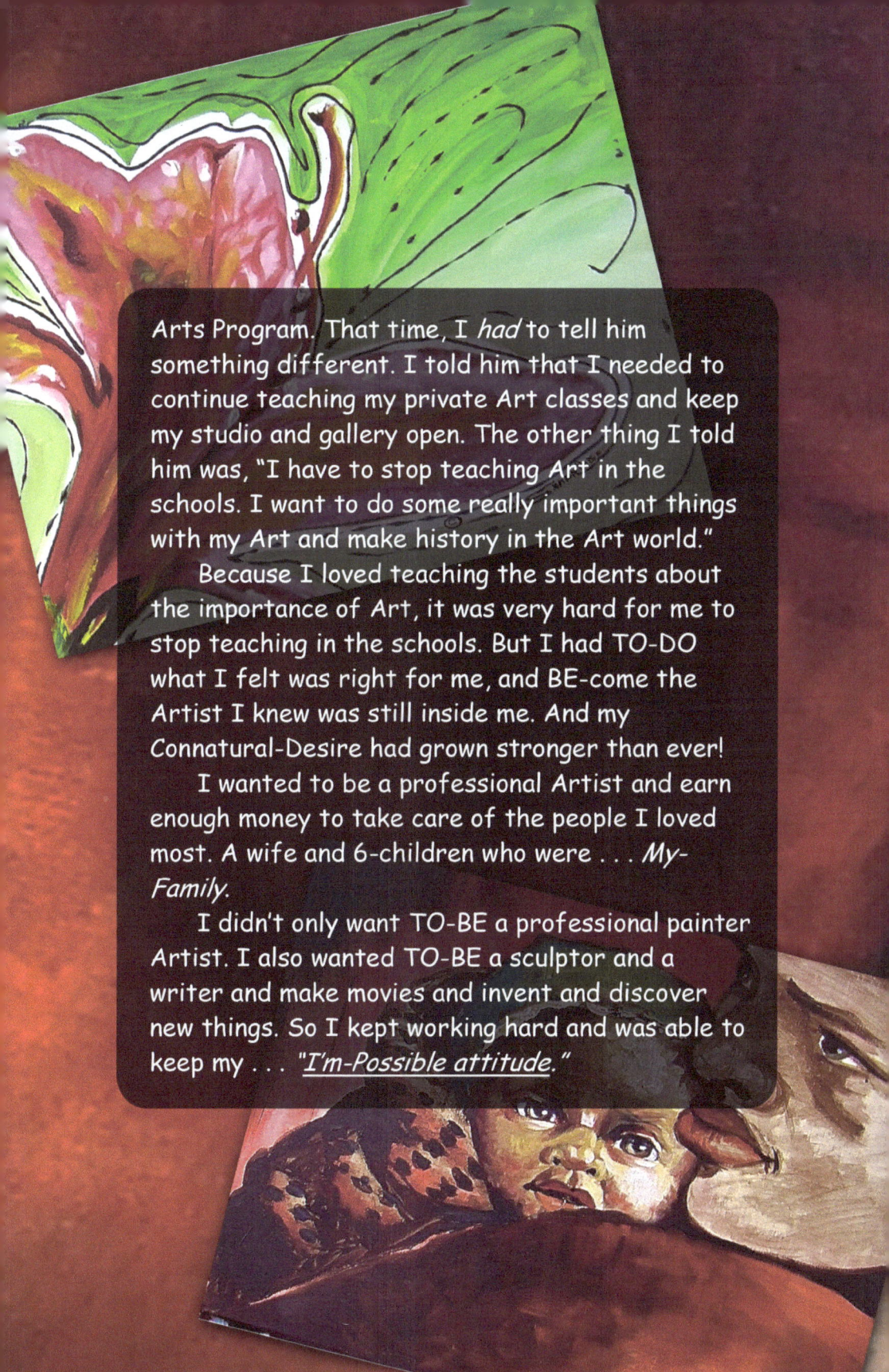

Arts Program. That time, I *had* to tell him something different. I told him that I needed to continue teaching my private Art classes and keep my studio and gallery open. The other thing I told him was, "I have to stop teaching Art in the schools. I want to do some really important things with my Art and make history in the Art world."

Because I loved teaching the students about the importance of Art, it was very hard for me to stop teaching in the schools. But I had TO-DO what I felt was right for me, and BE-come the Artist I knew was still inside me. And my Connatural-Desire had grown stronger than ever!

I wanted to be a professional Artist and earn enough money to take care of the people I loved most. A wife and 6-children who were . . . *My-Family.*

I didn't only want TO-BE a professional painter Artist. I also wanted TO-BE a sculptor and a writer and make movies and invent and discover new things. So I kept working hard and was able to keep my . . . *"I'm-Possible attitude."*

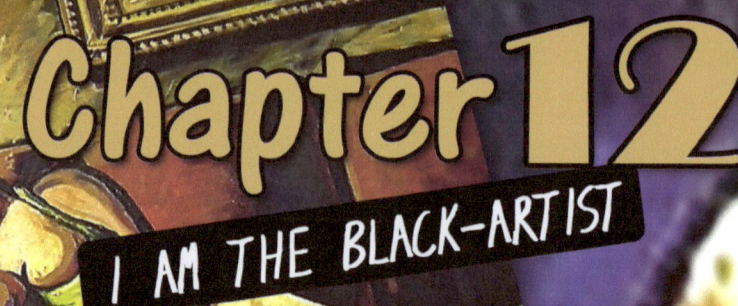

Chapter 12

I AM THE BLACK-ARTIST

My Connatural-Desire Gland grew stronger **and stronger** from age 28 to 32. But my body was weaker because I had abused it by smoking cigarettes and drinking alcohol and taking drugs. I became so sick I almost *died*. I couldn't create Art anymore, and had to live in the bedroom most of the time.

My sickness forced me to hide my face in my hands. That way I could see THE CREATOR OF LIFE'S face in my he<u>art</u>.

And . . . I . . . *lived*.

I was 32-years old and BE-came a certified Naturopathic Doctor. I started living a healthier life and regained my health. Then my Connatural-Desire Gland pushed me TO-BE and TO-DO more. So I said with my m<u>ind</u> and he<u>art</u>, *"I am ready TO-BE a famous Artist and TO-DO great things with my Art and TO-HAVE fun."* I started creating Art again and loved it more than before.

When I was 39-years old I had a very, very strong Connatural-Desire Thought. My strong thought was, *"Santa Claus is a White-Man. I don't feel Black-People need to make Santa Claus look black . . . what if Santa had a best friend . . . who is* a Black-Man?"

So?

I used my *IMAGINATION* to *IMAGINATE* and *IMAGINATED* Santa Claus's very Best-Friend and named him . . . *PAPA-CAUSE™*.

I wrote a 32-page picture book and titled it *PAPA-CAUSE™ The Friend of Santa Claus*. I drew and painted the pictures for the book, and also wrote songs about him. A very special friend dressed up as PAPA-CAUSE™. He sang the songs and danced and talked to Children and Teenagers in schools and community centers in Alabama and Georgia. When my friend couldn't dress as up PAPA-CAUSE™, I did. Children and Teenagers of all races from all around the world saw and loved PAPA-CAUSE™.

From the age of 38 to 39, every day I worked really hard to BE-come a famous Artist by painting and sculpting and writing.

At 43-years old I made history with the Coca-Cola Company. I was "The-First" Artist the company ever allowed to use their name and logo to paint Black-People in happy paintings.

I also wrote a book about my great-great-grandfather. His name was Nimrod. The title of that book is *Red Book and Cotton*.

Yes, I did that and much, much more.

I made history, *but* most people in the world have never heard of or read about me . . . not yet . . . but *they will*.

THE CREATOR OF LIFE gave me some very important things to share and say to the world. I must DO-IT*.

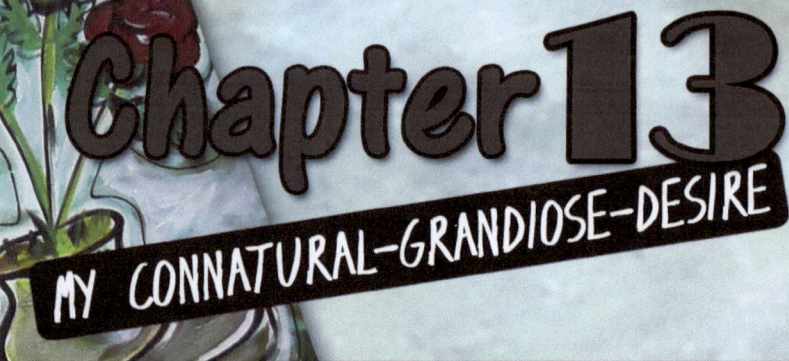

Chapter 13
MY CONNATURAL-GRANDIOSE-DESIRE

I must be honest with you. My Connatural-Desire Gland is *really, really, really, very strong*. When I was a child I wanted TO-BE a cartoon Artist. When I was a Teenager I wanted TO-BE a musician. When I was a young man I wanted TO-BE a professional painter Artist and sculptor and make history with my Art. When I was an older man I wanted TO-BE an author. Today I want TO-BE and TO-DO 3-Greater Things. The 1st thing is TO-BE "The First" Artist to *show* Children and Teenagers how to use IMAGINATION so that "They Will Save Their Own Future" from *The Nasty-Stuff-Family* created by Adult-Greed. The 2nd thing is to build a school where Children and Teenagers are taught and sh<u>own</u> how to use IMAGINATION and create a better world for all people. And the 3rd thing is to tell the world that IMAGINATION came from . . . *The Original Black-Africans.*

    I was 59-years old and it was January 2010. My Connatural-Desire Gland gave me the *big-super-push*, which was a Connatural-GRANDIOSE-Desire, my greatest desire ever.
    The word grandiose means, aim high and BE

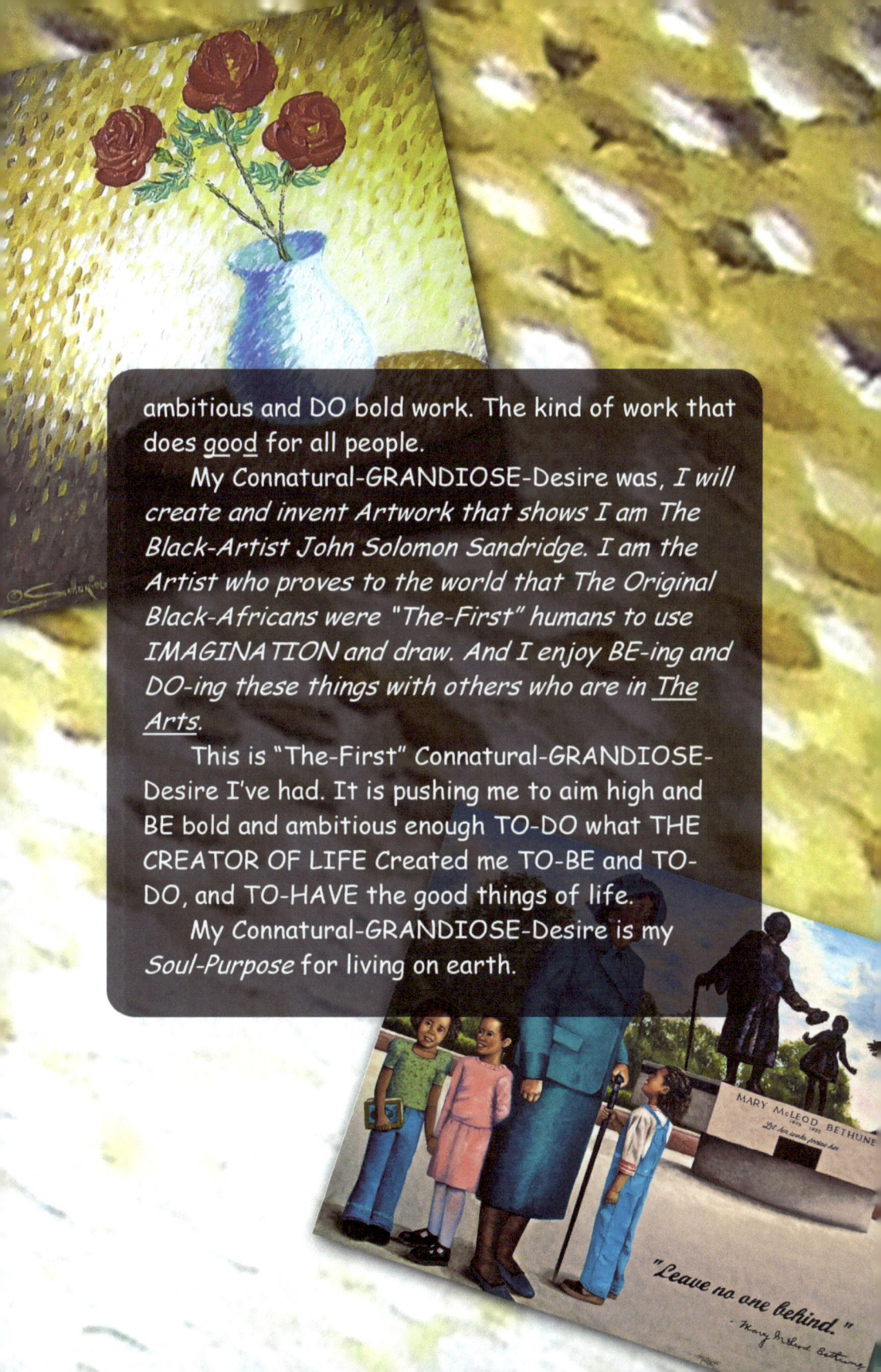

ambitious and DO bold work. The kind of work that does <u>good</u> for all people.

My Connatural-GRANDIOSE-Desire was, *I will create and invent Artwork that shows I am The Black-Artist John Solomon Sandridge. I am the Artist who proves to the world that The Original Black-Africans were "The-First" humans to use IMAGINATION and draw. And I enjoy BE-ing and DO-ing these things with others who are in <u>The Arts</u>.*

This is "The-First" Connatural-GRANDIOSE-Desire I've had. It is pushing me to aim high and BE bold and ambitious enough TO-DO what THE CREATOR OF LIFE Created me TO-BE and TO-DO, and TO-HAVE the good things of life.

My Connatural-GRANDIOSE-Desire is my *Soul-Purpose* for living on earth.

MARY McLEOD BETHUNE

"Leave no one behind."
Mary McLeod Bethune

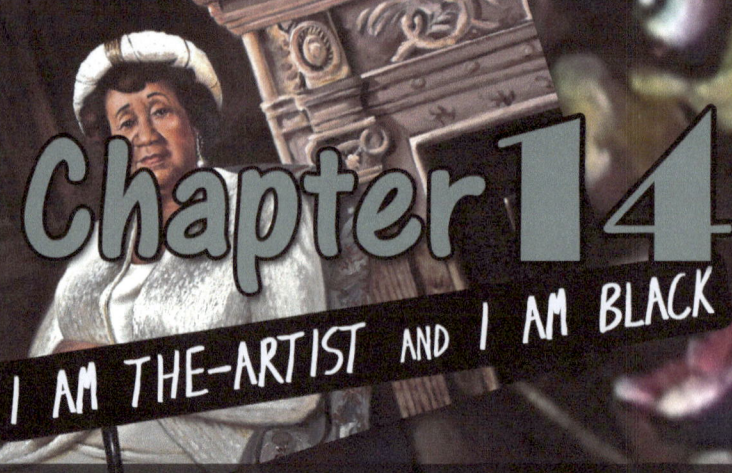

Chapter 14

I AM THE-ARTIST AND I AM BLACK

May 10, 2011 I was 61-years old. That day I prayed and meditated and thought . . . _"I am Black. I am an Artist."_

That was the first time in my life I knew for sure that my _Blackness_ was GOoD. I used my IMAGINATION, and allowed THE CREATOR OF LIFE to tell me the name of "The-First" new Art form I would invent. The name is . . . _NUMINOUSNEOISM™ ART._

From April 2011 to January 2012 I used my new Art to _IMAGINATE_ and paint over 100-paintings.

A QUESTION.

What kind of Art is NUMINOUSNEOISM™ ART, and can other people create this kind of Art?

The ANSWER.

Yes, yes, yes.

NUMINOUSNEOISM™ ART is Art that's _alive_. It lives because the Artist puts his or her spirit into it. And the Artist can be any age, which means _all_ Children and _all_ Teenagers can use their REAL-MAGIC and IMAGINATION to IMAGINATE their very own

NUMINOUSNEOISM™ ART.

NUMINOUSNEOISM™ ART is 1-word with 3-parts and 3-meanings. The way to say NUMINOUSNEOISM is *Nuw – Me – Nous – Ne – O – Is – Um.*

The 1st part is *NUMINOUS* (Nuw-Me-Nous) and it means: drawings or paintings or collages or sculptures or music or dances or songs or poems or stories or plays or movies or technological art that's filled with the presence of THE CREATOR OF LIFE.

The 2nd part is *NEO* (Ne-O) and it means: the Artist's feelings and ideas are new and recent and different and spiritual.

The 3rd part is *ISM* (Is-Um) and it means: unique feelings and expressions that come to the Artist from THE CREATOR OF LIFE who is The-Source of all creativity and inventiveness and discoveries, which makes people reconnect with each other and The-*Source of all life: THE CREATOR OF LIFE.*

The simple meaning for NUMINOUSNEOISM™ Art is: Art that comes to earth through *any Artist* who has the "I'm-Possible attitude." The Art is created "First" by the CREATOR OF LIFE in the heavenly place. THE CREATOR OF LIFE puts the Art into the mind and brain and heart of the Artist through their IMAGINATION. Then the Artist *IMAGINATES* the Art through his or her hands and feet and mouth and body as drawings or paintings or collages or sculptures or music or dances or songs or poems or stories or plays or movies or technological art, and the Art is TO-BE GOoD for everyone and the earth.

When I create my NUMINOUSNEOISM™ ART I feel THE CREATOR OF LIFE working through my mind and brain and he<u>art</u> and eyes and feelings and emotions and thoughts and hands and body. I will SHOW Children and Teenagers HOW to use IMAGINATION to IMAGINATE a better life for themselves, and a better world for everyone.

I am . . . the only Human-BE-ing who will do the work of my Connatural-GRANDIOSE-Desire, and only THE CREATOR OF LIFE can make it come true in me and through me.

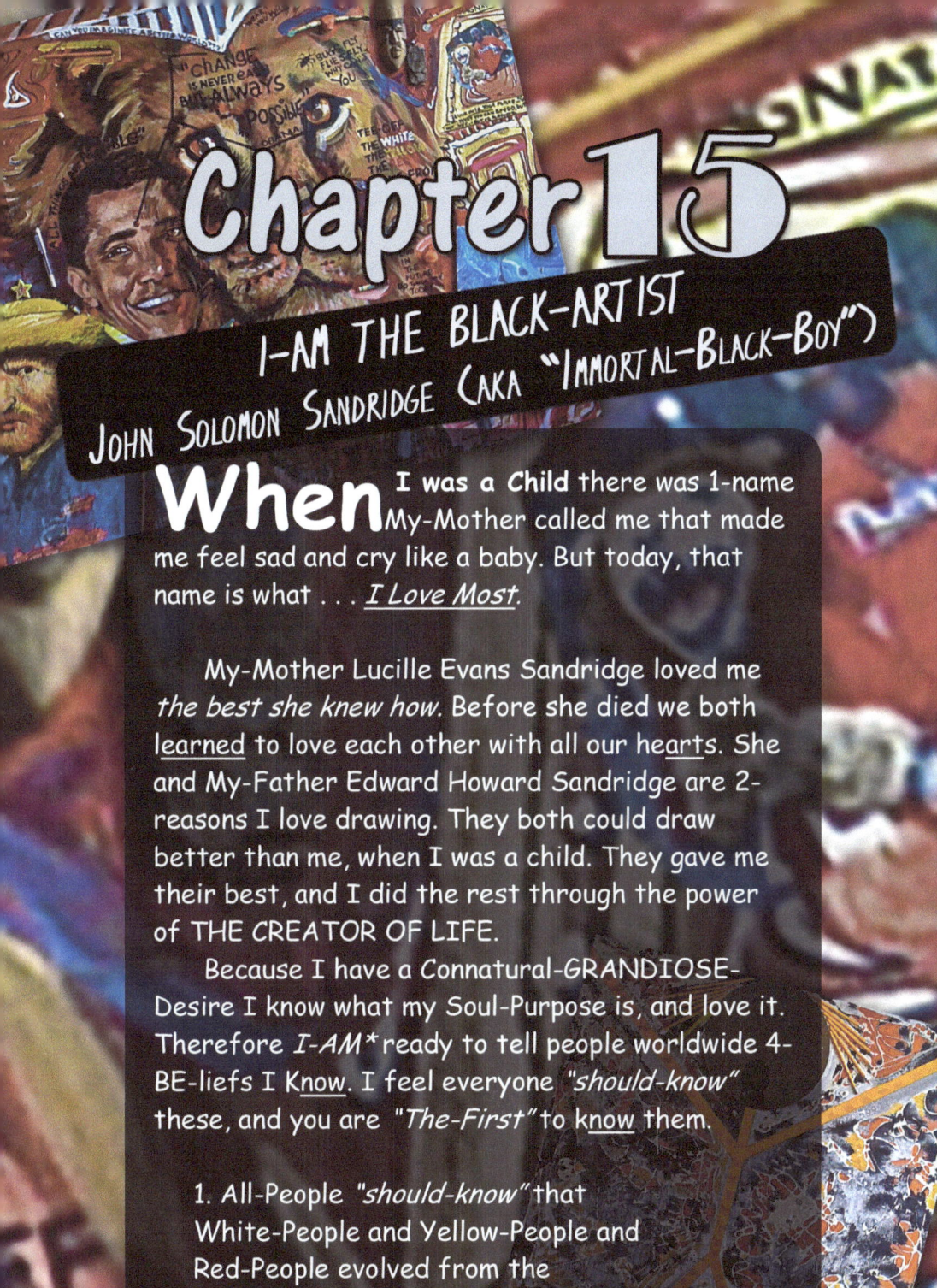

Chapter 15

I-AM THE BLACK-ARTIST
John Solomon Sandridge (aka "Immortal-Black-Boy")

When **I was a Child** there was 1-name My-Mother called me that made me feel sad and cry like a baby. But today, that name is what . . . <u>*I Love Most*</u>.

My-Mother Lucille Evans Sandridge loved me *the best she knew how*. Before she died we both <u>learned</u> to love each other with all our he<u>arts</u>. She and My-Father Edward Howard Sandridge are 2-reasons I love drawing. They both could draw better than me, when I was a child. They gave me their best, and I did the rest through the power of THE CREATOR OF LIFE.

Because I have a Connatural-GRANDIOSE-Desire I know what my Soul-Purpose is, and love it. Therefore *I-AM** ready to tell people worldwide 4-BE-liefs I K<u>now</u>. I feel everyone *"should-know"* these, and you are *"The-First"* to k<u>now</u> them.

1. All-People *"should-know"* that White-People and Yellow-People and Red-People evolved from the Original Black-African-People who were "The-First" humans to live on earth.

2. All-People *"should-know"* IMAGINATION and DRAWING came from "The-First" humans who were the Original Black-Africans.

3. All-People (especially Adults) *"should-know"* all Children and Teenagers are TO-BE *"The-First"* humans to use the NO. 2 Pencil and REAL-MAGIC and IMAGINATION, and *"They Will Save Their Own Future"* from Adult-Greed: Pollution, Poverty, Sickness, and War.

4. All-People *should-know* "The-First" drawings and paintings and stories and music and dances came through the IMAGINATION of "The First" humans . . . the Original Black-African-People who lived in Africa.

This is all true.

I WILL *SHOW* Children and Teenagers *HOW* to use IMAGINATION and "They Will Save Their Own Future" from . . . *THE NASTY-STUFF-FAMILY.*

Now I'll tell you the name My-Mother called me that made me feel sad and cry like a baby. When I heard those 2-words come out of her mouth my he<u>art</u> hurt really, really bad.

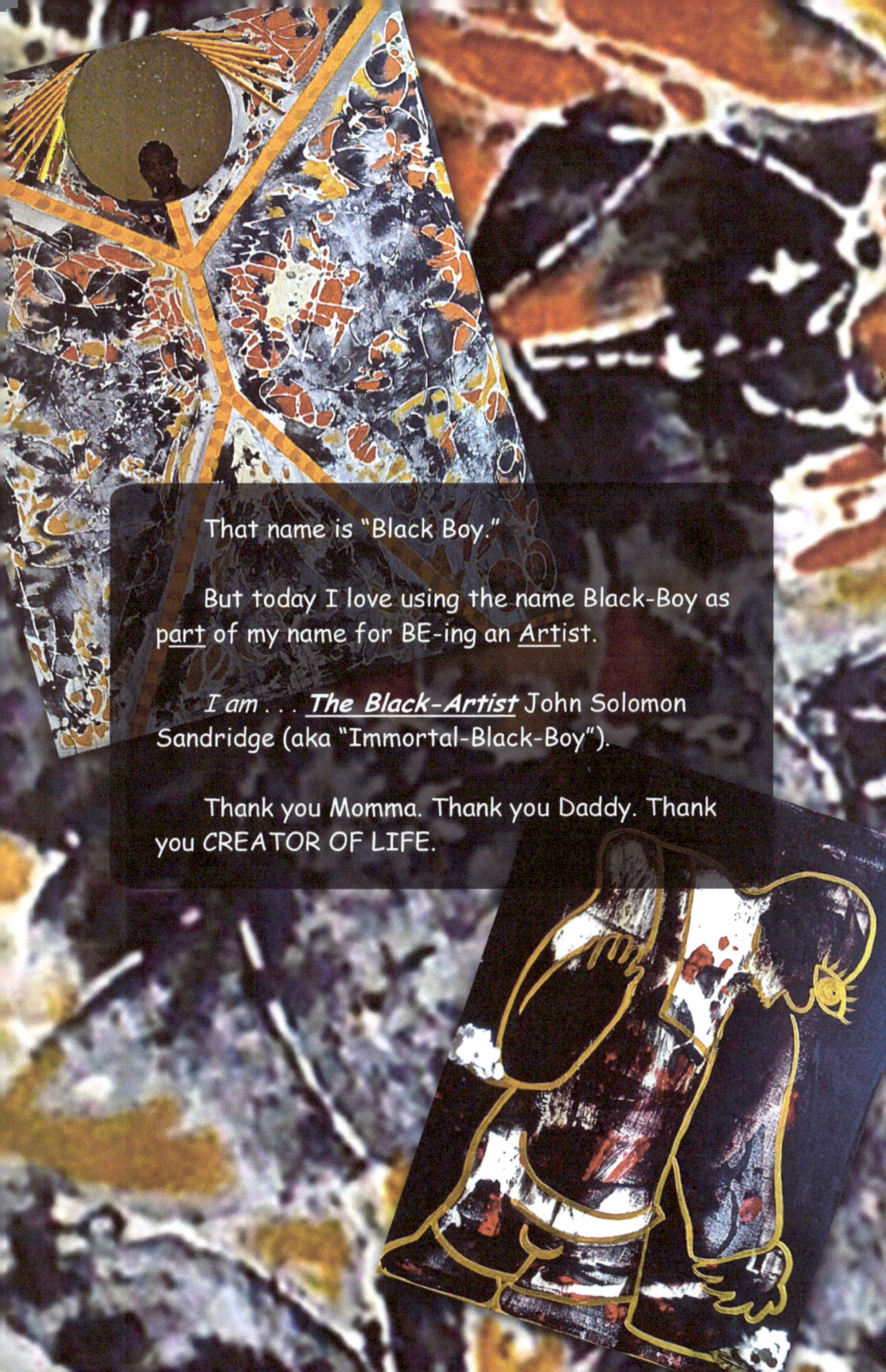

That name is "Black Boy."

But today I love using the name Black-Boy as part of my name for BE-ing an Artist.

I am . . . **The Black-Artist** John Solomon Sandridge (aka "Immortal-Black-Boy").

Thank you Momma. Thank you Daddy. Thank you CREATOR OF LIFE.

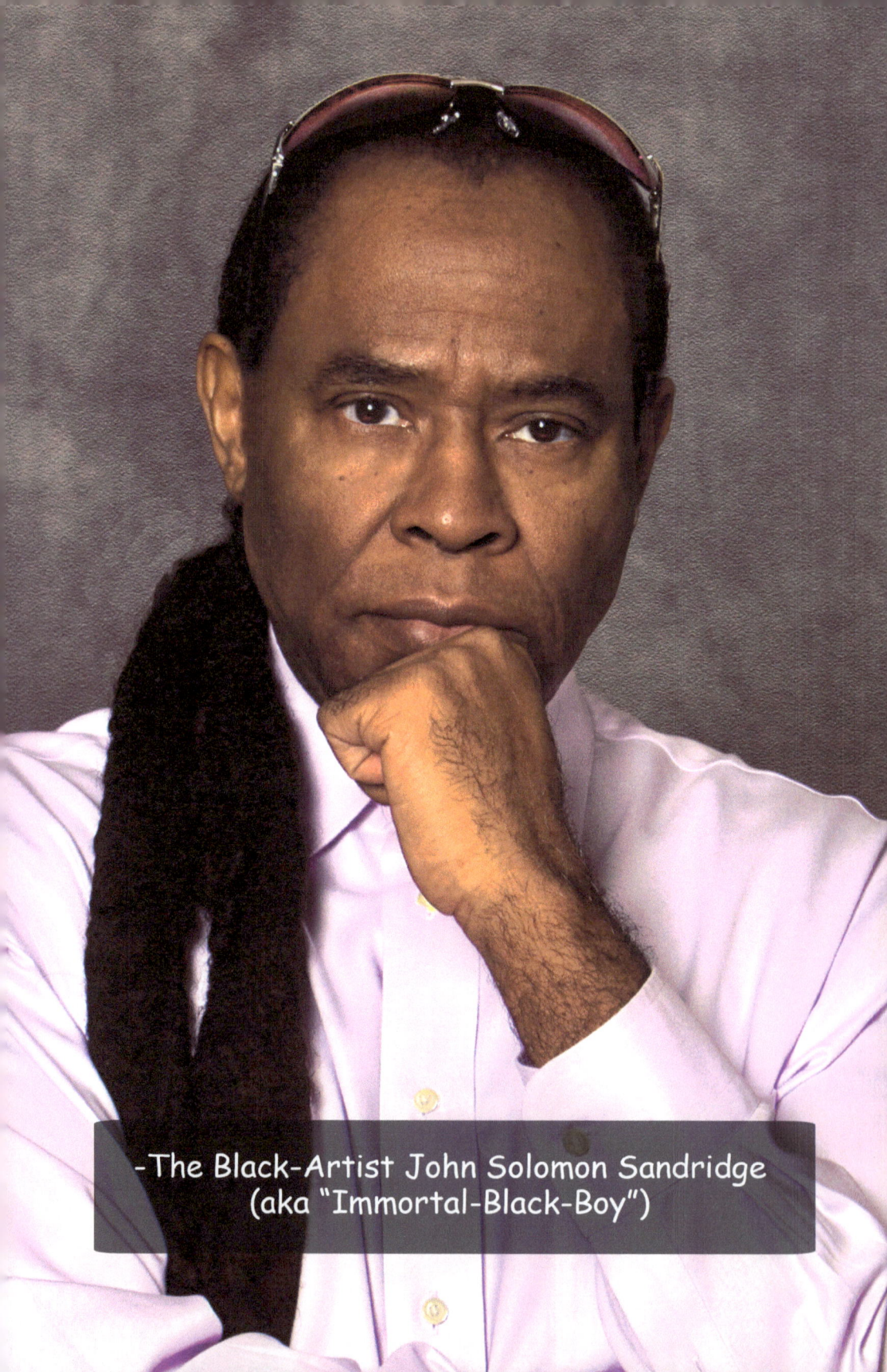

-The Black-Artist John Solomon Sandridge
(aka "Immortal-Black-Boy")

WORDS INVENTED BY
THE BLACK-ARTIST JOHN SOLOMON SANDRIDGE (aka "Immortal-Black-Boy")

Adult-Greed: 21st century adjective-noun: someone who is a grown-up that is selfish and has an excessive desire for more of everything and cannot and will not use it all during their lifetime.

BE-come: 21st century verb-verb: living with desire and putting effort in living a life that is the great-journey given by THE CREATOR OF LIFE.

BE-Lies: 21st century verb-intransitive verb: acting out something learned (believed) that is not accurate or true.

BE-lieve: 21st century verb-intransitive verb: living with desire and putting effort TO-BE and TO-DO what you were created by THE CREATOR OF LIFE TO-BE and TO-DO.

BE-living: 21st century noun verb-adjective: living with desire and putting effort in living the purpose-life THE CREATOR OF LIFE created you to live.

BE-GOoD: 21st century noun-adjective: living in a way that is agreeable to the best interest of all life on earth and the earth itself, which is the divine-way to live.

BE-ING: 21st century noun verb-noun suffix: a person who lives what they know to is true for them; I am to a great or greater degree everyday in everyway.

CONNATURAL-DESIRE: 21st century adjective-verb: a single desire that comes out of countless desires which are present at birth and which is developed without instruction; the need TO-BE and TO-DO things with excitement, passion, and strong love.

Could-BE: 21st century verbal auxiliary, past of can-verb: able to live the purpose-life THE CREATOR OF LIFE created you to live.

DO-IT: 21st century verb-pronoun: make something come into the world and happen that has its own life and reason for BE-ing.

GOoD: 21st century noun-adjective: a supreme divine-way to BE and DO what you were created to DO and BE and HAVE.

good: 21st century noun-adjective: divinity expressed reliably and satisfactorily in every way.

Heart-Dream: 21st century noun-noun: love and emotional courage to live and BE and DO a goal that is a purpose-life.

I-AM: 21st century pronoun-pre 1st singular of BE (intransitive verb): you BE-ing the great person you are inside.

IMAGINATED: 21st century transitive verb: the end result of imagination having brought a never-before seen and unknown into earthly reality: philosophy, idea, concept, invention, discovery, or arts.

IMAGINATE: 21st century adjective: the result of imagination having brought a never-before seen and unknown into earthly reality: philosophy, idea, concept, invention, discovery, or arts.

IMAGINATING: 21st century transitive verb: the process of using the imagination to bring a never-before seen and unknown into earthly reality: philosophy, idea, concept, invention, discovery, or arts.

IMAGINATION: the Spiritual Eye of the mind that humans use to see creations and inventions and discoveries in Heavenly-Places, which THE CREATOR OF LIFE formed as human-potentials.

IMAGINATOR: 21st century noun: the person using their imagination to bring a never-before seen and unknown into earthly reality: philosophy, idea, concept, invention, discovery, or arts.

I'M-POSSIBLE: 21st century noun-adjective-verb: a person who believes and knows "They Can BE and DO All Things" because THE CREATOR OF LIFE Creates in them and through them by way of their P-P: Personal-Potential.

IMPOSSIBLES: 21st century adjective: things and situations and conditions a person cannot and will not let happen to them and for them because of their fear-based beliefs (BE-Lies one has <u>learned</u> to live).

MAGICALLY-MIRACULOUS: 21st century adverb-adjective: the enchantment of supernatural divine intervention in human affairs by way of spiritual law.

Peace-full: 21st century noun-adjective: calmness and harmony and togetherness with yourself and others.

Power-filled: 21st century noun-verb transitive: the strong ability TO-DO and TO-BE.

POWER-FULL: 21st century noun-adjective: the spiritual ability to produce boundless creativeness and inventiveness and discoveries that have GOoD effects on all people.

REAL-MAGIC: 21st century adjective-noun: objective, independent, genuine, and actual supernatural artful existence.

THE NASTY-STUFF-FAMILY: the family created by Adult-Greed, coming from the dark side of adults who do not remember how and why to love and share.

The-Now: 21st century definitive article-adverb: BE-ing and DO-ing in this very moment.

TO-BE: 21st century prepositional-verb: movement in BE-ing the one who lives and breathes the life of humanness into their work and play.

TO-DO: 21st century prepositional-verb: movement in BE-ing the one who brings never-before seen and never-before heard creations and inventions and discoveries from heavenly-places into material/physical existence.

TO-HAVE: 21st century prepositional-verb: movement towards acquiring or getting possession of and using <u>GO</u>o<u>D</u> things for one's service and sharing it with others.

Would-BE: 21st century verb-adjective: strong wishful desire and effort to live a GOoD life.

"Immortal-Black-Boy": when I was a child my Mother called me black boy when she was anger. Because I have forgiven her, and I love her, today I choose to keep the name "Immortal-Black-Boy" forever.

Definition of
NUMINOUSNEOISM™ ART

Definitions are the invention of The Black-Artist John Solomon Sandridge (aka "Immortal-Black-Boy")

NUMINOUSNEOISM™ ART: 21st century noun: To-Be filled with the (numinous) presence of The Divine; having spiritual feelings and ideas that are (neo) new and recent; a different form or manner of processing and presenting one's (ism) actions and behavioral characteristics as expressions of THE CREATOR OF LIFE BE-ing expressed as ART through the Artist, who is a creative human-BE-ing who adheres to the *doctrine of Oneness (unified quality of wholeness)* and the *theory of religious (religion:* Latin roots re—again and ligare—to bind, bond, bridge, and means to bind together again, to re-late, heal the wounds of separation which cannot be affixed to one side of any opposites: men-women, daylight-night, right-wrong, black-white*)* Universal Creative *Principle (fundamental law; rule; code*) of BE-ing and DO-ing one's Divine-Purpose.

Forms of NUMINOUSNEOISM™ ART

LIVING-ART: 21st century adjective-noun: Art incorporating the mystical-magic of mirrors reflecting the feelings and emotion of the viewer. Without judgment, willingly absorbing its surroundings; it is totally open to receive whatever and whoever stands within its view; taking on their life and reflecting the paradox of being human: playful and serious, pain and pleasure, retaining the beauty and ugliness of humanity, showing the viewer the world/their world in the moment, NOW.

PERSONALLY-PRIVATE Art: 21st century adverb-adjective: Art created specifically for the individual. It contains personal items that make a statement about their life and/or profession; their unique way of BE-ing and DO-ing in the outer-world; a reflection of their inner-world. (Client provides items – clothing, etc. – and I present a palette of colors they can choose from.)

PARADOXICAL-ART: 21st century adjective-noun: inspires viewer's wholeness in BE-ing human; viewer automatically goes within and reflects on inner thoughts and feelings, walking away with a diffused subjective view about the clarity of objective reality.

ANTINOMY-PORTRAIT ART: 21st century plural-noun: fundamental representation of one's irresolvable conflict and contradiction with inner beauty and ugliness; a paradoxical statement of personal-humanness. (Antinomy: a contradiction between two apparently equal valid principles or between inferences correctly drawn from such principles; irresolvable conflict or contradiction; a paradoxical statement, such as beauty and evil and slavery and freedom.)

SUPERFLUITY-STUFF ART: 21st century plural-noun: Art created from whatever, and means no-thing but many-everything.